More Praise for
TEENS with the COURAGE to GIVE

"Although you wouldn't necessarily know it from today's headlines, America is full of young people like those in this book, who are doing remarkable things to make this a better world. After reading their stories, it's hard not to be optimistic about the future."

—SCOTT PETERSON, Executive Director, The Prudential Spirit of Community Awards

"How wonderful that organizations across the country are inviting young people, many of whom are living in very challenging conditions, to get involved and be a resource to their families and their communities. There are lessons here for youth workers, teachers, parents, and others who would doubt the power of young people, some quite young, to make a big difference in the lives of others while also developing their own potential."

—CARMELITA GALLO, Director, Program and Product Development, YMCA of the USA

"Jackie Waldman reminds us of an eternal truth that is often silenced by the din of an increasingly violent and valueless society . . . in giving we receive and by healing we are healed. Her poignant examples should inspire all of us to more vigorously seek ways to develop our most precious resource, our youth. The human spirit is such that when young people experience compassion, concern, and commitment from someone, they are better able to transcend life's mishaps. They will find "their place" and most often, they will settle in to a life of giving rather than taking."

—JULIE THOMAS, Executive Director, Volunteer Center of Dallas County

"Visit a high school for a day, and you'll leave with hundreds of stories of caring. This book brings teens' stories to life and helps us realize that they are all individuals with a limitless supply of caring and compassion. I can only hope that every adult will learn from this book and become involved in a meaningful way in the life of a child."

—Harold Brathwaite, Director of Education, Peel District School Board

"In helping others, we complete our healing. This often neglected truth is told with elegant simplicity and great sweetness in this touching book."

—James S. Gordon, M.D., author of nine books including *Manifesto for a New Medicine: Your Guide to Healing Parnerships, The Wise Use of Alternative Therapies,* and *Health for the Whole Person*

"This outstanding book shows teens through real-world examples that a true leader is a servant first. Leadership at its core is leaving the world better than you found it. I encourage all teenagers searching for answers to read this book."

—Hugh O'Brian, Founder & Chairman of Executive Committee Hugh O'Brian Youth Leadership

"*Teens With the Courage to Give* is a tribute to the determination of a very special group of young women and men to heal themselves. ANAD's Caroline Schramm and the other contributors to Jackie Waldman's book have much to be proud of, as they teach all of us that helping others to heal is the ultimate way to complete one's own healing process."

—Vivian Hanson Meechan, President and Founder National Association of Anorexia Nervosa and Associated Disorders

TEENS with the COURAGE to GIVE

TEENS with the
COURAGE to GIVE

Young People Who Triumphed Over Tragedy
and Volunteered to Make a Difference

JACKIE WALDMAN

Foreword by TOM CULBERTSON

CONARI PRESS
Berkeley, California

Copyright © 2000 by Jackie Waldman

All Rights Reserved. No part of this book may be used or reproduced in any manner whatsoever without written permission, except in the case of brief quotations in critical articles or reviews. For information, contact: Conari Press, 2550 Ninth Street, Suite 101, Berkeley, California 94710-2551.

Conari Press books are distributed by Publishers Group West.

ISBN: 1-57324-504-6

Cover Design: Ame Beanland

Cover Photos: Clockwise from left: Mededith Blake and Tessa Thompson: photo by Lena Ringstad 1999; Charlie Simmons: photo by Sgt. Pepper's Photography 1999; Allison Wignall: photo by Sumner Photography; Jeffery Rodriquez, Iris Serrano, and John Serrano of Latin Artists: photo by Pascale Craan of Youth Venture; Lo Dietrich: photo by Terry Dietrich 1999; Domingo Guyton, Jake Repp, John Wagner-Holtz. All photos courtesy of Jackie Waldman.

Book Design: Suzanne Albertson

Library of Congress Cataloging-in-Publication Data

Waldman, Jackie.
     Teens with the courage to give : young people who triumphed over tragedy and volunteered to make a difference / Jackie Waldman.
       p.   cm.
     Follow-up to : Courage to give.
     Includes bibliographical references.
     ISBN 1-57424-504-6
       1. Courage—Anecdotes. 2. Generosity—Anecdotes. 3. Voluntarism—Anecdotes. 4. Youth—Anecdotes. I. Title.

BJ1533.C8 W257 2000
179'.9—dc21
                                                   99-059297

Printed in the United States of America on recycled paper.

00 01 02 03   RRD   10 9 8 7 6 5 4 3 2 1

In blessed memory of Zachary Bell, Farra Bloom, and all the teens whose lives ended too soon, I dedicate this book. May we always remember their smiles, their laughter, how they made others happy—their courage to give.

To laugh often and much,
to win the respect of intelligent people
and the affection of children,
to earn the appreciation of honest critics
and endure the betrayal of false friends,
to appreciate beauty, to find the best in others,
to leave the world a bit better,
whether by a healthy child,
a garden patch, or a redeemed social condition;
to know even one life has breathed easier because you have lived.
This is to have succeeded.

—Ralph Waldo Emerson

TEENS with the COURAGE to GIVE

]F YOU ARE LIKE ME, YOU HAVE SAT THROUGH SEVERAL GRADUATION ceremonies where the speakers try to inspire the students by telling them that they are the hope of tomorrow. If there is one thing that I have learned in working with young people through Youth Service America (YSA), it is that young people are really the hope of *today*.

Each day, millions of kids across our great nation give back to their communities by feeding, teaching, planting, protecting, mentoring, nurturing, coaching, cleaning, and caring in service to others. No country on earth even comes close to the phenomenon of the American youth service movement. Remarkably, volunteering by young people is growing in popularity and continues to set new records of participation and levels of sophistication. Support is coming from adult champions such as parents, teachers, business leaders, and politicians. Peer pressure from youth themselves is also a huge factor.

One of the most profound messages of Martin Luther King, Jr. is that "everybody can be great, because everybody can serve." Wow! Every young person deserves to feel greatness during their adolescence, regardless of their physical attributes or their athletic and academic abilities. Service to others brings resilience to kids, equalizing what is a challenging and even isolating time of life.

But the youth service movement is more than just beneficial to the participants. Last year, teenagers alone contributed an estimated 2.4 billion hours in time to their communities. In particular, youth serving other youth in schools, agencies, parks, hospitals, libraries, museums, and on athletic fields had a powerful impact on health care, education, and community development. Interestingly, the majority of adult volunteers in America first started volunteering in their youth. With adult service valued at over $255 billion to the U.S. economy, this makes the youth service movement a critical pipeline to the economic and social stability of the United States.

Youth Service America is the umbrella organization for hundreds of programs, large and small, in schools, congregations, and agencies across the country. Our mission is to strengthen the effectiveness, sustainability, and scale of the youth service movement. What that really means is that we want to make service to others the common expectation of every young person as they grow up in the United States. Just as graduation from high school has universal acceptance, YSA believes that every student should have the opportunity to give back to others and their communities.

Among YSA's programs is National Youth Service Day, which was started in 1989 to give annual recognition to the amazing things young people do every day in service to others. It is now the largest service event in the world! YSA also has a major site on the Internet called SERVEnet (www.servenet.or http://www.servenet.org) to tap into the power of technology and reach young people in cities, rural areas, and the suburbs. In order to increase the number of volunteer "slots" available, YSA created the Fund for Social Entrepreneurs to underwrite six new organizations a year created by recent college graduates. To recognize the sheer hours of time given by students ages five to twenty-five, YSA also co-administers the President's Student Service Awards. This White House program moves "civic fitness" to the same level of recognition as the popular President's Physical Fitness Awards. For more information look at www.ysa.org.

As you read this amazing book by Jackie Waldman, you will meet individuals that represent literally millions of other young people who have discovered the importance, fun, and value of service to others. You will also learn one of the best kept secrets in the country: In spite of isolated incidents and provocative stories about teenagers in newspapers and on television, the vast majority of young people in America are more kind-hearted, helpful, law abiding, reverent, and intelligent than the media wants you to know. Read on, and let each of these stories inspire you to act.

Let him that would move the world first move himself.

—*Socrates*

THINK ABOUT THE MOST DIFFICULT DECISION OR CHALLENGE you are facing in your life. You may be dealing with a problem with a friend, an illness, the death of a loved one, culture identity, a learning difference, lack of parental support, an abusive dating relationship, adjusting to a new school, an eating disorder, peer pressure, a sick parent, substance abuse, poverty, or depression. Whatever you're faced with, it seems overwhelming, out of your control, and you don't know how to end the pain.

You may be asking yourself, "Why is this happening to me? I haven't done anything to deserve this. Why can't I have it easy like my friend does?" You may be experiencing gut-wrenching sadness. Or you may be feeling anger, like you're going to explode.

These are scary feelings. They lead to scary thoughts. Wouldn't it be amazing to know how to make yourself feel better? Wouldn't it feel awesome to have hope and joy in your life again? How great would it be to regain control of your life? Aren't you tired of the pain and suffering?

The teens you're about to read about have felt exactly like this, and they have found ways to transform their difficulties. Read their stories and go with them on their incredible journeys of self-discovery. Let them share their pain and their healing with you. They want you to experience what they have learned: When you help others, you help yourself.

Imagine that there's something bigger than you out there—that you're a part of something magnificent, that you matter in the grand scheme. Can you believe that your actions, your wisdom, and your heart can make a difference—that your courage to give can be part of the solution for a peaceful, loving world?

These teens show us that all that's required is to look courageously past your own problems for a moment. Reach out and help someone else, with all your heart and soul. You won't believe what happens. The problem you have seems easier to handle. And without even trying to solve your problem, you feel better than you have in a long time. That's because when you care about someone else and help create a better world, you're doing soul work—from within, feelings of happiness envelop you, crowding out your feelings of sadness. And when happiness comes from within, it lasts.

When I was diagnosed with multiple sclerosis in 1991, I was sad, angry, and scared. When I finally stopped spending my time looking for a cure that doesn't exist and started using my energy to help others, I experienced a fulfillment I had never known—so powerful that my feelings of sadness, anger, and fear have faded away. After having met teens whose lives have changed because they chose to help others, I wanted them to share their stories, so that you can see what's possible for you.

Tessa Thompson, one of the teens profiled, says, "The courage to give is the fuel to live." *Teens with the Courage to Give* confirms that you, our teenagers, are our teachers—you are our future. We adults must listen to your voices and see your visions for a safer, kinder world. Then together we can build it.

Kids Konnected

JON WAGNER-HOLTZ

WHEN I WAS NINE YEARS OLD, my mother was diagnosed with breast cancer. At that time we were living in a small town in Massachusetts, south of Boston. My mother's diagnosis was devastating to our family. We didn't know what it would mean in the long run.

Her illness was extremely tough for me. When she came home from the hospital after surgery, I felt it was my job to be strong for her. After her first chemotherapy treatment, she was very weak and sick to her stomach all the time. I was really angry. My mom was such a good person. How could this be happening to her?

But I never expressed my true feelings to her. I thought she had enough to worry about without having to worry about me.

Halfway through her treatments my dad was transferred to California; my mom, my sister, and I stayed in Boston so my mom could finish her treatments. My dad flew back and forth every two weeks for five months. It was hard on him not being with Mom and it was hard on us not having him home.

My mom noticed that I was not doing well with our situation. Thinking I would feel better if I could talk to someone, she sent me to a psychologist. Actually, I felt worse. I didn't like the idea that a professional had a preconception of what a child with a parent with cancer felt like. It felt like I couldn't be my own person.

I spent more and more time alone in my room. I was content playing with my Legos—they never talked back to me.

We finally made it through the treatments, and Mom started to regain her strength. She asked me to go with her to the Susan Komen Breast Cancer Foundation's annual Race for the Cure®. We went to the race, and Mom was up on the stage during the survivors' ceremony with about 300 other women wearing pink visors. Together they were celebrating life.

I thought at the time how great it was that she had such a tremendous support group. My next thought was that many of those women probably had children, and wouldn't it be great if all of us who had parents with cancer could have such a group?

I wrote a letter to the Komen Foundation in Orange County, asking them for funding to start a hotline that kids could call and talk to other kids who knew what it was like to have a parent with cancer.

They gave me $300 and 300 names of kids I could send letters to. I started the group, and I named it the Komen Kids.

I set up a twenty-four-hour hotline in my bedroom and started receiving calls. I probably got around a hundred phone calls, and there were eight or nine kids calling on a regular basis. We felt better knowing we were all experiencing anger, sadness, and fear.

One weekend I invited the eight regular callers to come to my house, and I brainstormed with them about my ideas for a support group. We wanted it to remain kids helping kids, but we knew we would have to have a psychologist with us.

Three of the other kids and I interviewed about eight psychologists, and hired one in a pizza parlor in Newport Beach. He understood that we wanted him with us for supervision, but that we wanted to run our own support group.

We decided our first meeting would be at the Disneyland Hotel in Anaheim. We wanted a place where kids could get away from the cancer environment. We knew that we couldn't have it at a hospital, because hospitals were viewed as the enemy by most of us. That's where our parents went and got sicker. At nine years old, we weren't smart enough to realize that in order for our parent to get better, he or she had to get sicker through chemicals.

Thirty-two kids came to the first meeting. Kids talked about their own situations, their feelings, and the problems they were having. One girl was crying as she told us she hated going home—how she hated seeing her mom throwing up, bald, and sleeping all the time, how she hated that the cancer invaded not only her mom but their entire family's life. Another girl sitting next to her gently took her hand to comfort her.

After that first meeting I felt better than I had since my mom was diagnosed. My own feelings were validated, and I knew the group meeting had helped the girl who was so upset. Helping another kid had helped me.

We sent flyers to doctors in Orange County to make sure as many kids as possible heard about our group. We were profiled in the media, and that really helped get the word out. As we grew I renamed the group Kids Konnected, and it became its own nonprofit organization. All our programs are free of charge. We're totally supported by donations.

Another chapter was started in Oklahoma City six months after our first meeting in Orange County. Now, six years later, we've got eighteen chapters around the nation in twelve states, ranging from West Palm Beach Florida all the way up to Vancouver, Washington. This year, with a budget of $300,000, we will help nearly 10,000 kids.

We also have summer camps, so kids can get out of the cancer environment. This year, the seven- to thirteen-year-olds went to Catalina Island to snorkel, swim, and bike ride. The fourteen- to eighteen-year-olds went whitewater rafting for four days. The camps are free of charge to kids, and if they're coming in from out of town, we provide a home stay for them and a day at Disneyland before they go to camp.

Another program is our Teddy Bear Outreach Group. We send teddy bears to newly diagnosed families. The teddy bear is a scruffy brown bear. We tie a ribbon around its neck and attach a card to the ribbon that says,

I'm just a little tattered teddy
With not a lot to do
Except to be a friend to comfort
Someone just like you!
If you're happy, sad, or have a tear
Just hug me, squeeze me,
And hold me near.
Lots of friends you can meet
When you call on the phone
They will always remind you that
You're not alone!

*"Friendship, Understanding, Education, and Support for kids
who have a parent with cancer."*
Kids Konnected

One day, Brian, one of our charter members, came to me and told me we needed to have a grief workshop. His mother had had cancer when we first started the support group and had since passed away. He said, "There needs to be more here for kids like myself who have lost a parent to cancer."

When Brian's mom died, his family put together a memorial fund for Kids Konnected and asked friends and family to donate to the fund in place of sending flowers. We used that money to start Karen's Kids, in memory of Brian's mom.

Four times a year, we send kids who have lost a parent to cancer to a six-week grief workshop. They learn how to deal with their pain and anger, how to say good-bye, and how to move forward with their lives. This is the only program the kids don't run. A psychologist does most of the work for the workshop.

But kids helping kids is the core of Kids Konnected. Adult volunteers supervise our program. We believe that the best way to help ourselves when we're in emotional pain is to help others. Our youth leaders attend monthly training sessions that teach them the skills necessary to be great facilitators. Every youth leader has had a parent with cancer, so they understand what the kids are going through.

At the group support meetings every month kids share their feelings, but they also learn more about the disease. A group may have a doctor come speak about chemotherapy. We also use art therapy during the support meetings. It's a comfortable way for kids to express themselves. If a group is fairly silent or hyper, an art project is great as an icebreaker.

Some kids stay in a support group a couple of months and feel they have gotten enough help. Others, whose parents are critically ill, may stay in the group until the parent passes away, and still others stay in the group for a year after their parent is gone. Some never leave. They want to help other kids the way they were helped, so they become youth leaders.

In addition to our hotline we have a web site where kids can go online to get information, e-mail us, and receive newsletters and meeting notices in their area. We also have a database on books about cancer and coping skills.

My favorite program is our support groups, because that's where the kids get the most help. That's where I got the most help.

I'm one of the fortunate kids. My mom is now an eight-year cancer survivor. She volunteers in the Kids Konnected office every day. When we've had a really great day—we know at least one child was helped—my mom will start to cry. She'll tell me how grateful she is to be here, alive, sharing these moments with me.

I spent my high school years working hard to reach as many kids as possible. I would take classes at school in the morning and arrive at the office at 12:30 each day. As graduation approached and I knew I would be leaving for college in the fall, I started training other students to take over running the day-to-day office duties.

McDonald's gave me a $50,000 scholarship and named me the nation's top entrepreneur for creating the hotline—a hotline that more than 6,000 kids use to express their feelings and challenges. I have received other awards and scholarships—among them a Prudential Spirit of Community award and scholarship, a React Take Action scholarship, and a National Caring Institute Award—making it possible for me go to college at Slippery Rock University in Pennsylvania. I'm a freshman majoring in political science and minoring in community-service learning.

I will be forever grateful for the healing power of Kids Konnected. The success of the program lies in the tears of a child being wiped away by a caring friend and in the quiet "thanks" of a sick parent who can worry less about the emotional stress their illness has on their child. Kids helping kids is what we're all about. Because of our "Konnection," a child does not have to be alone anymore.

"Friendship, understanding, education, and support for kids who have a parent with cancer." Contact: Kids Konnected, P. O. Box 603, Trabuco Canyon, California 92687. Tel: 714-380-4334 or 800-899-2866. Fax: 949-582-3989. Web site: **www.kidskonnected.org**.

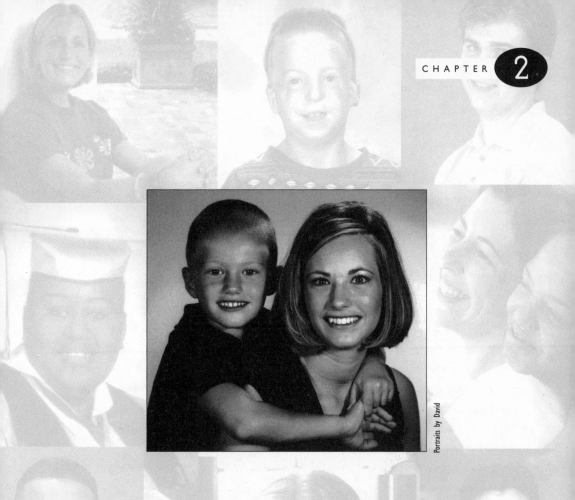

CHAPTER 2

Portraits by David

From the Eyes of a Child

RONNA VAUGHN

I THOUGHT MY BOYFRIEND HUNG THE MOON AND THE STARS. By the time I was fourteen, we were having sex—I did whatever I could to make him happy. I loved him with all my heart.

The day after Christmas I told my mother I needed to talk to her. She was cooking supper and said she didn't have time. I said, "No, Mom, we need to talk now. You need to sit down." That's when I told her I thought I was pregnant. I was in eighth grade.

Her first question was by whom. Then she said, "Never mind, I know who." She left the room and didn't say anything else to me about it for a few days.

We went to the doctor a few days later. I was three months pregnant.

I had often had irregular menstrual cycles, so when I missed my period in November it didn't really worry me. Some of the time my boyfriend and I had not used protection, never thinking anything could happen. But when I missed my period in December I started to worry. When the doctor told us I was pregnant, I started crying right there. My mom cried too. It was horrible.

I told my boyfriend and he said he would be there for the baby—no matter what happened with us.

Two weeks later, I learned that my best friend was pregnant by him, too. He didn't deny it. I cried myself to sleep every night. I was a total wreck.

I never really thought that an abortion was the right thing to do. My parents are divorced, and when my mom and I went to my dad to tell him I was pregnant, his first word was *abortion*. He said he would pay for me to have an abortion. My mom wanted me to have one too. Out of respect for them, I did think about it. But

I told them I couldn't. My mom was really crushed. But she was supportive. From that point forward she made sure I got the prenatal care I needed.

I went to school up until the last six weeks. The teachers gave me work at home and I turned it in, and they graded it. If I needed help I called a teacher or one of them came to my house and helped me.

At this time—in my eighth month—my grandparents were getting sick and needed somebody to help care for them. My mom bought a house next door to theirs to be there for them.

I was glad to be moving. My boyfriend lived right across the street from me. Before I got pregnant we were together all of the time. But now he avoided me.

I was taking a shower at my grandparents one night when I felt a sharp pain. Grandma called my mom next door, and she took me to the hospital right away. The next day, July 22, 1994, I had my son, Robbie. He weighed eight pounds, four ounces. I was fifteen years old.

Mom called my boyfriend to tell him, but he never showed up to see his child. I decided right then that it was his choice—I wouldn't ask him again to see his child.

The Department of Human Services in Knox County Tennessee assigned a PARTNERS case manager to me. I don't think I would have made it without them. PARTNERS is a teen-parenting service that uses an intensive case management approach in the home, school, and community. I received individual counseling and emotional support and supportive services such as child care, transportation, medical services, and referrals. As long as I was in school and attended weekly group meetings, PARTNERS paid for a percentage of my child care.

I started back to school when Robbie was only a month old. I wasn't even old enough to have a driver's license. Mom picked me up after school, drove me to daycare to get Robbie, and took us home.

I fed him, bathed him, did my homework, played with him, and put him to bed—every day. Sometimes I'd be up until 1 A.M. or 2 A.M. making bottles and doing homework. And I had to get up the next morning at 5:30 A.M. just to get myself ready and then get him ready and off to daycare so I'd be on time for school.

I didn't have many friends. Everybody knew me; everybody was nice to me, but I didn't have any close friends. They didn't want to drag a baby around.

All I had time for was school, work, and Robbie. At lunch the girls talked about the weekend parties, shopping, makeup, clothes, and after-school activities. I listened to them and thought I was never going to get to buy new clothes like the other girls. I had to buy diapers. I was never going to have new shoes like everyone else. Robbie needed shoes.

I finally quit eating with them and went to the school office to visit with the principals—I had more in common with them than anyone my age.

I got my own apartment my senior year. Robbie and I needed our own space. After school I worked at a dry cleaners until 7 P.M. Then I'd go get Robbie from my mother. She picked Robbie up from day care every day. My paycheck was spent before I even got it. I paid $300 in rent and $320 in childcare. Then I had to buy food and pay the bills—electricity, phone, and water.

One day, our school had a teen fair with lots of different nonprofit groups represented. One nonprofit group, the Florence Crittenton Agency, Inc., was recruiting for a program called STARS (Students Teaching and Respecting Sexuality). STARS is made up of teens who have had children and teens who have chosen to abstain from sex.

I knew right then I wanted to join. If I could prevent one teen from having to struggle as I have, then it would be worthwhile.

STARS promotes abstinence. I speak to middle school and high school students and tell them the benefits of abstinence. I tell them I have made the choice not to have sex again until I'm married. I tell them that if they made a bad choice to have sex they can make a good choice to stop. I give them facts about pregnancy, sexually transmitted diseases, and contraception, and encourage them to consider the consequences of their behavior and make their own choices.

I share my story. I tell them I made the choice to have sex, and I made the choice to have Robbie, so it was my responsibility to take care of him—a consequence I have to live with.

I tell them how my mom asked me, when I first got pregnant, how I would take care of a child. I said to her, "I don't know, but I'll love him." It's true that you can love a child—and I do love Robbie so much—but no matter how much you love your baby, love will not buy diapers, it will not put food on the table or a roof over your baby's head.

I talk about all the things I missed—football and basketball games, going to the mall with friends, after-school activities—things so important in a teen's life.

I also volunteer for PARTNERS because their emotional and financial support was so important to me. After meeting with Tennessee state legislators who were working on new welfare reforms, I was even elected chair of a new advisory board.

We focus on educating parents. A lot of parents don't know how much teens must face when they go to middle school or high school—peer pressure, sex, drugs, and alcohol.

Last year I went to Atlanta for the Georgia Campaign for Adolescent Pregnancy Prevention. I told my story and afterward answered questions from parents, teachers, and adults—questions about my parents' reaction, if I ever had time to be with friends, how I dealt with it.

I easily could give up. At times I am so exhausted. But Robbie keeps me going. I always thought I wanted to do something good with my life, but when I had

Robbie—somebody else to be responsible for—I knew I had to get the best education possible and work harder than ever. What kind of life would Robbie have if I just gave up?

He has started asking questions, like, "Who is my daddy?" I tell him honestly. I say his name and I say that he was somebody I used to date but don't see anymore. He asks me if he can see him. I tell him maybe one day.

I used to be so angry. I wanted to blame my boyfriend. But we both had something to do with me getting pregnant—I was just the one who took the responsibility for my actions.

I'm not angry anymore. Being angry doesn't get you anywhere; it doesn't accomplish anything. Now I think of ways to help others—ways to prevent teen pregnancy. I'll be happy if I make a difference in one girl's life and she doesn't have to grow up before she's through being a child.

If you're a teen mother and need assistance or know of someone who could use guidance contact: PARTNERS, 901 East Summit Hill Drive, Knoxville, Tennessee 37915. Tel: 800-445-6538.

If you're at risk or in crisis and want to achieve your highest potential, contact: The Florence Crittenton Agency, Inc., 1531 Dick Lonas Road, Knoxville, Tennessee 37909. Tel: 423-602-2021. Fax: 423-602-2039.

Learn more about teen pregnancy prevention. Contact: National Campaign to Prevent Teen Pregnancy, 2100 M Street NW, Suite 300, Washington, DC 20037. Tel: 202-261-5655. Web site: **www.teenpregnancy.org**.

A Peaceful Warrior

DOMINGO GUYTON

I GREW UP IN A VERY LOVING HOME IN BOSTON WITH MY MOTHER and grandmother. Alcohol, drugs, swearing, abuse, and neglect were issues I never experienced at home. On Saturdays I went to choir rehearsal at our church, and we went to Sunday School and church every Sunday. My mom read Bible verses to me every day. I never had any problems with these two beautiful women.

Walking out of my house was like entering a different world. The guys in the neighborhood were "hardcore"—fights, drugs, and gangs dominated the streets. Every day someone got shot or stabbed.

One night another guy and I got beaten up. I was only twelve years old. Fifteen guys came after us. They actually let me go; the other guy was beaten up really badly.

After the incident the guy who was badly beaten never spoke to me again. He felt I ran out on him and left him to get killed. I was just trying to protect myself. I saw an opportunity to get away and I had to take it.

Three years later this guy's friends decided to retaliate because they felt I didn't help defend the guy when we both were attacked. They were still angry about something that happened when I was in the seventh grade.

We started having little fights on and off. My mom would get mad at me for fighting and punish me. She tried talking with me and forbidding me to go places, but I just kept fighting.

I ended up getting jumped one day by fifteen guys. I got hit in the head with a metal object and had to get six stitches. This was in May 1990.

In November of the same year I ended up getting stabbed four times by the same group. I was stabbed twice in my right arm, once under my right arm, and once in my right leg.

I was with a friend when it happened. We were on 8th Street when they attacked me. I didn't want my mother to see me bleeding so I walked all the way down to 25th Street to a friend's house. I sat on his front steps while he called for an ambulance.

I stayed in Boston City Hospital for three days. While I was there a man named Mark, from the Violence Prevention Project, came to visit me. We had a few great conversations about youth violence. He really helped me with my anger and fear while I was there. But when I left the hospital I felt very unsafe. Mark had given me his business card and told me to keep in touch, but I never did.

I heard the guy who stabbed me was taken to the Department of Youth Service, a place for offenders under the age of eighteen. But all his friends were still on the streets. I decided if they wanted to play hardball, I'd play. I was ready to retaliate.

I went out and purchased some protection. I carried a gun with me any time I was out on the streets. I was so angry I couldn't see what was happening. All that I hated and feared about those guys—their violent nature and unreasonable grudges—were now characteristics that fit me. I was no different than my enemy.

I began selling marijuana with some of my friends on my street. The guys on the next street over accused us of taking their customers. So now I had new problems with another group of guys. Little fights were happening all of the time. It became us against them wherever I went.

These little wars resulted in me having to go to court. Those other guys selling drugs accused me of shooting at one of them. They said the bullet went through a window of somebody's home.

While I was waiting for my court case, I was ordered to begin therapy. I was hooked up with a man named David, a black man who was a positive role model. He wanted me to talk about the incident and talk about my anger and fear. After we met for a few times, he came to the conclusion that my problems may have stemmed from not having a father in my home. He told me he had a good friend by the name of Ulric Johnson he wanted me to meet.

At the time, Dr. Johnson was the director of the City of Boston's Department of Health and Hospital Gang and Drug Prevention Program. He also teaches at Harvard University.

Dr. Johnson saw the need to start a youth-based program that would provide primary gang and drug prevention education and intervention services to youth service providers, youth, and families in the city of Boston.

So, in 1990, Dr. Johnson created TAGV—Teens Against Gang Violence. The program is comprised of youth of color from different cultural and ethnic backgrounds, both male and female, ranging in age from fourteen to twenty.

Dr. Johnson came to see me and told me something I'll never forget. After getting to know me, he said I had many positive qualities and that underneath all my anger was a person who was capable of great things, but also a person who was afraid of his future. He said I wasn't the type of person who needed to go to jail. He told me he would help me if I would let him.

That was the turning point in my life. Dr. Johnson came to court with me. He spoke on my behalf to the judge. The case was dismissed because they couldn't find the gun—they had no evidence. But the judge told me if he ever saw me in court again, I'd be gone. He wanted to put me away this time, but without evidence he couldn't.

The court case showed me how close I had come to throwing my life away. It scared me enough to want to change—but I had no clue where to begin. Miraculously, Dr. Johnson believed in me and offered me the tools for change.

I was fascinated with this man. His calm demeanor and quiet confidence were qualities that seemed foreign to me. With him I felt a comfort and safety I had never felt outside of my home.

He told me TAGV members are trained to conduct workshops at schools and churches on violence prevention, gang violence prevention, and cultural diversity. Members help in the community, go to retreats together, and visit other programs.

He said the main cause of violence is the failure to appreciate the many diverse aspects of ourselves and others, including color, culture, class, character, and context. He called these the "5 Cs of awareness." He said he believed nonviolence can be achieved, but only if we value our differences and support peace and justice.

He also said that TAGV believes that through our confidence, courage, commitment, development of community, and willingness to face conflict—the "5 Cs of change"—and embracing the *Nguzo Saba,* the seven principles of Kwanza, we would be able to achieve peace and justice.

I wanted to know more about the seven principles of Kwanza, the principles guiding this peaceful man. He told me the principles were *umoja* (unity), *kujichaguli* (self-determination), *ujima* (collective work and responsibility), *juamaa* (cooperative economics), *nia* (purpose), *kuumba* (creativity), and *imani* (faith).

He looked at me and said, "Domingo, true peace is not the absence of violence, but the presence of justice."

I liked this man and his philosophy. It wasn't enough to end acts of violence. They had to be replaced with acts of kindness. Sitting back and doing nothing would not create peace.

After meeting Dr. Johnson and becoming involved in TAGV, I got into one more fight. In October 1991, my junior year, I got kicked out of the private school I was attending. The principal had warned me if I got into one more fight he'd kick me out.

I had to change schools. But Dr. Johnson never gave up on me. He seemed to know it would take a while for me to give up all the anger within me. It wasn't going to happen overnight.

Dr. Johnson showed me the consequences of violence. He reminded me that friends of mine were spending time in jail and that one of my friends was sent to prison for life.

Once again, Dr. Johnson let me know he believed in me. He asked me if I would speak to other youth about nonviolence even though he knew I was change in progress. Every time I told my story, I learned more about myself. I was helping others but really helping myself.

As I spent time expressing my feelings and talking to others about the "10 Cs," I realized I was beginning to live a life of nonviolence. My anger was slowly burning away as a sense of purpose and peace enveloped me.

I quit fighting in 1993. The need was gone. Working with young people, helping out in the community, and appreciating my family became my priorities.

I started writing songs about the realities of life. Recently my first CD was produced. I have since graduated from college with a degree in health services. I work in a residential home for at-risk teenage boys. Most live there because of their violent natures. I tell them, "Look out for yourself, because nobody else is going to look out for you. You think the world owes you? The world owes you nothing. You better work for it, and if you're hanging around on street corners you won't see anything. If you go ahead and hang, you'll learn the hard way. When you're sitting in the Big House and you're rotting in that cell, rotting away, you're going to remember the day I talked to you. Matter of fact, that's going to be my prayer— you can't say that you weren't ever told, because I'm telling you right now. If you mess up, I pray that while you're sitting there, you're going to think of me telling you this day that there's another way to live."

Embrace the 10 Cs. Bring TAGV's message to your school. Start a chapter of Teens Against Gang Violence. Contact: Teens Against Gang Violence, 2 Moody Street, Dorchester (Boston), Massachusetts 02124. Tel: 617-282-9659. Fax: 617-282-9659. Web site: **http://tagv.org/geninfo.htm**.

Find out about other violence prevention programs. Contact: National Crime Prevention Council, 1700 K Street NW, 2nd Floor, Washington, DC 20006-3817. Tel: 202-466-6272. Fax: 202-296-1356. Comments about the online resource center can be directed to **webmaster@ncpc.org**.

For more information about our activities or publications, you can contact the Council at this address: National Crime Prevention Council, 275 Sparks Street, 5th Floor, Ottawa, Ontario KLA OH8. Tel: 613-941-9306. Fax: 613-952-3515. E-mail: ncpc@web.net. Web site: **http://crime-prevention.org/ncpc**.

CHAPTER 4

Terry Dietrich 1999

It's What You Do with What You Have

LO DIETRICH

WHEN I WAS THREE MONTHS OLD, I WAS DIAGNOSED with a disease called cystic fibrosis. Not much was known about the disease at that time—fifteen years ago—so I can just imagine how scary it was for my parents. I've never known what it would be like to live without this disease, but I do think about how much fun it would be to get up one morning and run outside to play. I realize that will never happen—I will never experience that kind of freedom.

Cystic fibrosis (CF) is genetic. I was born with it. It's not something I caught from the air like you catch a cold or the flu. It's not something that will go away like they do either. CF affects everything that goes on inside me, especially my lungs and pancreas.

In a normal pancreas, enzymes are directed to food to help it break down and be used by the body. But my pancreas is blocked because of cystic fibrosis. I have to take enzyme capsules every time I eat in order to digest my food.

In normal lungs, mucus is thin and slippery, but in people with cystic fibrosis, it is thick and sticky. Because of this congestion, it is hard for me to breathe in and out. The congestion also contains bacteria that causes pneumonia, which I get several times a year.

One of the keys to feeling good is to get as much mucus out of my lungs as possible. So, I do three hours of physical therapy and breathing treatments every day. I have a machine called a "Thair-a-vest®" to do the physical therapy. It looks like a life vest hooked up to a box about the size of a window air conditioner. I wear the vest and turn on the box. The machine in the box makes the vest vibrate and shakes my body to help loosen the mucus so I can cough it out. Actually, the whole house shakes when I do my therapy!

Then I have to breathe different medicines into my lungs to help kill the bacteria and open up my airways so I can breathe easier. So far, I can't say that the medicines taste anything but horrible.

All this stuff takes a lot of time out of my day. I wish I could skip it but whenever I do, I get even sicker and have to take more medicine. I already take about fifty pills a day. Besides, whenever I get sick, that means I may spend three or four weeks in the hospital or on IVs—a tube that carries medicine and goes up in your arm about twelve inches. Ouch!

I know that the hours I spend doing all my CF treatments takes away from the time I would like to spend with my friends. Many nights I go to bed kind of sad, wishing I could just get up the next day and be a normal kid. But I can't. The biggest challenge of my disease is the fact that I know neither it nor the pain I live with will go away. I have to do everything I can to keep fighting so I can enjoy every day of the life I am living.

In spite of having a life-threatening disease, I think life is pretty grand. I'm very blessed to have a wonderful support system. I have the greatest mom and dad and big sister. They have given me a warm, loving home life. One of the best medicines is knowing how much they care. My sister, Jane, keeps me laughing. When I'm feeling sad, helpless, or frustrated, I know without a doubt that Mom, Dad, and Jane are there for me, along with my grandparents and other family members.

I also have lots of friends. When I get sick and miss stuff, they still call me and tell me what happened at a party or a school activity. They come to visit me all the time when I'm in the hospital. My hospital room is always filled wall-to-wall with cards and balloons and stuffed animals. My friends are really, really special to me. I've heard about other kids who have problems and don't have many friends. Sometimes people even make fun of them. My friends are just the greatest.

I accept what I have. I know I can't change the fact that I have cystic fibrosis. Instead of sitting around feeling sorry for myself, I stay busy trying to keep up with my friends, playing sports, and raising funds for CF so kids in the future who have this disease will have a cure.

One of our family's favorite events is called Great Strides, sponsored by the Cystic Fibrosis Foundation. It's an annual nationwide walk that local CF chapters host. My mom and I co-chaired Great Strides in Tulsa last year, and my dad and Jane helped.

We decided to reach out to the youth in our city to participate. Since 91 cents of every dollar goes directly to research, the more kids involved, the better. The executive director of the Sooner Chapter of the Cystic Fibrosis Foundation, JoAnn Winn, and the director of special events, Jan Jackson, loved our idea. Jan worked directly with us to help make our idea a reality.

When we first spoke with school administrators, we told them that we knew many schools have community service requirements, and we thought this was a great way to help meet them. We also mentioned that this was an avenue for students to participate in a worthy cause to offset recent events involving youth violence in schools.

Two of the schools were already participating because each had a student who was also a CF patient. At all of the schools we recruited a teacher, parent, or administrator. Knowing what their own school community service needs were, they helped adapt the plan to their particular school.

We went to each school and spoke to the students in an assembly. We handed out brochures to everyone who was interested. Several schools came up with great ideas to motivate kids. In one elementary school, two moms challenged a couple of homerooms to see which class could raise the most money. The moms treated the winning class to an ice cream party in their classroom. One eighth-grade teacher told her students that if they had 100 percent participation, everyone could skip their final exam. A CF board member sent letters to student leaders from several schools inviting them to attend an informational meeting. From that meeting a mother and daughter volunteered to organize the effort at their school. The mom filmed her daughter interviewing me, and they aired the interview on the school's television network. Another dad recruited the student council and class board members of his kids' high school.

We tried to think of every way we could to raise the most money. We made sure all the leaders knew about matching funds in which corporations will match student-collected funds. We trained students to look for answers about CF in the brochures on which they wrote the donations they collected. We showed students an example of how easy it was to collect money by asking neighbors, parents, and grandparents, and even by donating money they'd earned themselves from baby-sitting or other odd jobs.

When the day of the event finally came, we were excited but nervous. We'd worked so hard and wanted everything to go well. We hoped to raise thousands of dollars and have hundreds of kids participating, knowing they were helping find a cure for a deadly disease. We wanted them to feel good about what they were doing.

We were not disappointed. The day was a miracle. I'll never forget all of the kids, teachers, parents, and administrators who met at the zoo to turn in the money they had raised. They couldn't possibly realize how much hope each one of them gave me and every other cystic fibrosis patient who came to the walk, let alone the patients who fight CF every day all over the world. All together, the money raised in Tulsa totaled more than $150,000 for research!

Any student from any school district in the country can experience what it feels like to help save a child's life—to help find a cure for cystic fibrosis. My mom and I have written a step-by-step plan for any student to bring Great Strides to their city. Included is everything you could possibly need—how to recruit school leaders, forms for corporate matching funds, press releases, and more. We'll send it to you for free.

My philosophy of living depends on three things. First, I spend lots of my time fund-raising. I don't spend time worrying about how sick I could become, about dying. I may die when I am thirty, but I also may die in a car wreck today. So I'm not going to spend time worrying about it. I'm leaving that part to God. I think God holds each of us in His hands. If He wants to take me up to Heaven with Him, then He will.

Second, I think that your heart is where your faith is. If it's with God, then you'll be happy. If your faith is in yourself, money, or clothes, then that's all you have to depend upon to hold you up. You have to carry it all.

Finally, it's not what you have; it's what you do with what you have that makes your life better—or worse. I think life is like a board game. Sometimes you roll a bad day and sometimes a great day. Just remember when you only roll a one, with God's help, you'll soon roll a six.

Years from now, when I look back on my life, I think I'll feel good. I'll know I didn't spend the years just letting others take care of me. I'll know I didn't waste time feeling sorry for myself. I'll know I did spend time raising money to help find a cure for CF. I'll know I lived my life helping others, and that's a really cool way to live.

Be the student in your district who starts Great Strides. Be the student who can say, "I helped find a cure for cystic fibrosis. I helped save a child's life." Contact: Cystic Fibrosis Foundation, 6931 Arlington Road, Bethesda, Maryland 20184. Tel: 1-800-FIGHT CF. Web site: **www.cff.org**.

CHAPTER 5

Home Is Where the Heart Is

NIESHA SUTTON

] THOUGHT THE WORST PART OF MY LIFE WAS LIVING WITHOUT MY FATHER. He's in prison and has only been out once for a short period of time since I was born. We hardly know each other, but it's not from my lack of trying. I wrote to him and sent him pictures of me. He only wrote me back a couple of times, and that was a long time ago.

I love my dad, so it's not easy on me. I'm hoping that when he gets out of prison I can get to know him. I'll try again.

For most teens, having a father in prison would be enough to have to deal with. The day the ceiling in our home fell in proved far worse.

Last year we lived in a rented house, and the landlord neglected the repairs. When the ceiling fell in and destroyed the house, my mom called the landlord. She didn't even care—she didn't offer to move us to a different house or fix the roof.

Part of the ceiling fell on me. My left ankle and leg were very swollen. I couldn't walk on it for two weeks. The ceiling also hit my neck, so I was in a neck brace for weeks.

But the physical pain was nothing compared to the pain of not having a home and not having money to move anywhere else.

Suddenly my mom, my five brothers and sisters, and I were homeless. We had to pack our things and go to the Office of Emergency Shelter Services in Philadelphia.

That night was the most terrible night ever. All sorts of people were in one big room filled with cots. I looked around at all the men, women, and children with their own sad stories. I lay there mad, scared, and heartbroken. How could the landlord treat us like this? How could our lives change so quickly? Just that morning I lived in a home like most families, and now I was in a homeless shelter. I started to cry and couldn't stop. I was crying for me, my mom, and my brothers and sisters—maybe even for my dad.

I was in seventh grade and loved my school and friends. Our home was the place all the kids came to—my mom always let my friends spend the night on weekends. My home was fun, comfortable, and safe. How could this be happening?

The next morning the people who ran the shelter found us a permanent shelter to move to. The shelter was far away from our old neighborhood. When I saw the middle school near the shelter I suddenly realized I lost more than a home. I wouldn't be able to go to school with my friends anymore. As we drove up to the shelter, tears poured down my face. I couldn't help it.

I didn't want to go in—I never wanted to spend another night in a shelter. But, I also knew we had no choice.

The director took us to our rooms. At least it wasn't one big room. The shelter was an old nursing home with sixty rooms. They gave us two rooms and told us we could stay there as long as we needed to.

My sister and I shared one room. My mom, my brothers, and my other sisters took the other room. Bathrooms were at the end of the hall. I would be sharing a bathroom with strangers. When I walked into the bathroom to look at it, I about died. For a thirteen-year-old girl who needed privacy, this was a living nightmare.

At first I spent all of my time in my room. I hated the place. I didn't know anyone and I didn't want to meet anyone. I kept thinking we wouldn't be there very long. I kept hoping.

There were strict rules to follow. It was hard following someone else's rules when I was used to living in my own home with our own rules. But I did what I was told. I knew my mom didn't need me to cause trouble—she was upset enough.

I was required to join the teen group—a group of kids between the ages of thirteen and eighteen living in the shelter—and go to meetings every Wednesday from 6 to 8 P.M. with the youth case worker, Miss Pat.

The first meeting I went to was an "anger" meeting. I listened as other kids talked about their feelings. One girl said she was ready to hurt herself because her mom was getting on her nerves and she had to watch her little sister all of the time. Miss Pat told her she was glad she could express her feelings and let out her anger.

I noticed how much better the girl felt having the other teens and Miss Pat's support. I wanted to tell Miss Pat how mad I was at the landlord, how much I missed my friends, and how much I hated living there, but I couldn't do it. Just then Miss Pat reminded us that if we couldn't talk about our feelings, we could write to her in the journals she had given us.

I wrote a long note to Miss Pat letting her know how I felt. The next day when I opened my journal I saw that she had written me back. She told me to keep expressing my feelings and asked me to join in the teen activities at the shelter and at my school so I could get to know the other kids.

The kids at my new school were very friendly. I've never had trouble making friends anyway, so I made new friends really quickly.

The school is in an area of big homes with the shelter around the corner. So I knew my friends lived in really nice homes. When they asked to come over to my house after school, I told them I would have to ask my mom. The next day I would tell them my mom was busy and said maybe another day would be better.

I would stay after school until 6 P.M. I would sit at the bottom of a hill on the school grounds until every kid was gone. Then I walked home to the shelter. I never let one kid know where I lived. I was embarrassed.

Miss Pat helped me adjust to life at the shelter. I'm really glad I listened to her because we're still here—ten months later. I haven't given up hope that we will move to our own home again soon, but I can now say my life here is okay.

We have pizza parties and movie nights. We get to go on field trips to the aquarium, museums, and parks. Miss Pat makes sure we have fun.

She has taught us about respecting ourselves. We have to dress properly, come downstairs with our hair fixed, and respect our elders. If the older residents are rude to us, we're taught to be polite anyway and not make their problems our problem.

Every night we eat dinner with our own families, but Fridays we dress up and have a special dinner together. Our clothes are donated so everyone looks real nice.

When new families come in, the little kids need help. They usually don't act very well because they don't know the rules and the routine. Miss Pat has each of us in the teen group "adopt" one child. We take the kids out to the park and to the movies. We help them at the shelter too. Then we write in our journals what we did to help our child adjust to the shelter and have fun.

Helping the little kids has changed my life at the shelter. I am so busy helping them with their homework and helping little babies learn to walk and talk that I forget to worry about my own problems.

I also realize that if I feel sorry for myself I will be letting my brothers and sisters down. They're young—they don't care where they live. They're happy. I don't want them to learn to feel bad about living in a shelter, to learn embarrassment, so I hold my head high. I'm trying to make it the best I can for them.

My mom feels so badly for us. This isn't her fault—she never wanted us to end up living like this. I want to be strong for her too.

The shelter gave Mama an opportunity to finish her nursing schooling and internship, and she just got her first nursing job at a hospital.

We have applied for a new house. We filled out the paperwork and are waiting to hear if we get it. The caseworker tells us we should get to move soon.

I've asked Miss Pat if I can keep coming to the shelter after we move. I want to continue to help kids who first come into this kind of life. I want them to know that if they can follow the rules and learn to live in a group home, they can make it. They just have to hold their head high, reach out and help one other kid, and stick it out.

Miss Pat tells me I have really made a difference for these kids. She says she needs my help at the shelter, but she also needs my help with a new project. A camp is being started for the kids in the shelter called Kids Kamp and she asked me to be the teen advisor. The camp leaders want me to help plan activities and be a counselor at camp next summer. Homeless kids going to camp on the beautiful shores of New Jersey—now that's a miracle!

I'm excited to help. I'll have a chance to let the kids know the most important lesson I have learned. Home isn't really about having a roof over my head. Home is where my heart is—with my family and friends wherever I live.

If you are a child in a homeless shelter and would like information about Kids Kamp, or if you are someone who would like to start a Kids Kamp, contact: Kids Kamp, 4532 Frankford Avenue, Philadelphia, Pennsylvania 19124 Tel: 215-464-3955.

Learn how you can participate in an innovative grassroots project to raise awareness about homelessness and build support for the Education for Homeless Children and Youth program. Contact: National Coalition for the Homeless, 1612 K Street NW, #1004, Washington, DC 20006. Tel: 202-775-1322. Fax: 202-775-1316. E-mail: nch@ari.net.

CHAPTER 6

Mickey Pantano of New York City

An Oscar-Winning Performance

KIRSTEN LAWSON

As a kid I was pretty shy. I didn't have many friends in seventh or eighth grade, and by the time I got to high school I was one of those kids who hid in the corner behind a book.

I started coming out of my shell a bit during my senior year and got really involved in theater. I wanted to be an actress because then I could pretend to be somebody else.

When I turned eighteen, I thought, "Well, I'm an adult now and I can drink." I went from being totally anti-drugs and anti-drinking to becoming totally obsessed with drinking. I didn't feel as lonely, I didn't feel as weird, and I loved that feeling. I remember being home alone one night and calling a friend in Florida. I proceeded to drink and tell her about this wonderful discovery of mine. She got really scared and told me I should stop drinking then and there. I laughed in her face. Usually I was sensitive to people's feelings, but all of a sudden, I didn't care anymore.

It wasn't like I drank every day, so I didn't think I had a problem. I only drank when my family went away or on weekends. I couldn't wait to see the car leave so I could run to the liquor cabinet and get wasted.

When I graduated, I left for New York to study acting. I was scared to death of all the new people. At first I went to class, came home, and just locked myself in my room and studied. By second semester I started to focus more on the party scene and lost interest in my classes. My grades started to slide, and my teachers didn't know what to make of me. I kept screwing up in class all the time, and then I would start crying from the embarrassment. I put a lot of pressure on myself. It was becoming very uncomfortable to do anything sober.

I started smoking pot that same semester. At first I didn't try it because I thought it would ruin my voice. Then I did it one day and I found I could still sing the next day. I figured it was fine and smoked every chance I got.

I finished the semester—barely—and went home for the summer. I performed in a summer show; it helped keep me out of trouble, but as soon as the show was over I went back to drinking and smoking pot all the time.

My best friend lived in the next town over. One day I was sitting there getting stoned and she got really mad. She said, "Listen, you've got to pick right now—it's either this stuff or me."

I looked at her, and I had to think for about five minutes. Would I rather have the drugs or my best friend? Finally I swore to her I wouldn't do anymore stuff, blah, blah, blah.

But I was stoned the next night. This was scary to me. I was starting to wonder if I had a problem. When I made a promise to my friend and broke it the next day, I swore to myself I wouldn't touch anything anymore.

Things went well for a few months. My head was clear and I wasn't staying out all hours and hung over in the morning. I wasn't half-baked in class.

I started dating a guy, and we were getting along pretty well. One day he showed up with a bottle of brandy and a rose. We had some brandy and we did our thing. That was the first time I ever had sex with anybody, but as soon as it was over, I was more interested in the brandy than in him. I started making really cheesy excuses to get out of bed and get that bottle without him noticing.

From then on I was drinking, if not every day, pretty close to it. I was working part-time at a doctor's office. I was so hung over in the mornings I couldn't even file charts in alphabetical order. They finally let me go.

At school I had a teacher who told me if I took a dance class every day for a year, there was a good chance I could be on Broadway. This was my dream coming true. But I didn't say anything because all I wanted to do was spit in the guy's face. I knew I couldn't get high and go dance class every day. On some level I felt it wouldn't happen anyway so I decided not to try. I swore I'd never set foot on a stage again.

At this point if I didn't drink I was suicidal. I just couldn't stand to be in the same room with myself for more than five minutes without something in my system. I was in that much emotional pain.

I got to a point where the alcohol didn't stop the pain. I started looking for something stronger to take the edge off. I started using heroin and spent most of my time hanging out in Central Park. I was pretty miserable after a while so I decided to go back home to my parents. I really believed that when I got there they would take care of me and I would feel better.

I got home and spent three days lying on the couch, drinking and eating sleeping pills before I realized that I still wanted to die. I got scared. I ran into the kitchen and told my mom as much as I could about the drugs and alcohol. She had a friend in a twelve-step program who brought me along that very night.

I sat there feeling so afraid—afraid they wouldn't let me stay, afraid I wasn't bad enough. I didn't know how much I belonged there.

The meeting was small—all women. I remember everybody going around talking, and I cried through the whole thing. At first I was crying because I was so afraid. At the end I was crying because I didn't want to leave. It was the first time I didn't feel it was absolutely necessary for me to either slit my wrists or drink or get high. I felt safe with those women.

I tried to stop for a while but picked up again after a few weeks. I ended up in and out of detoxes and a halfway house. I lost jobs. I moved back to New York and crashed on people's couches until they got tired of looking at me. Then I'd move to someone else's couch.

One day, after being clean for almost three months, I decided I could have one drink. I found myself sitting behind a Dumpster in the East Village sharing needles with some guy I never met before, not caring if I lived or died. It wasn't like I didn't know about AIDS; it was more like, "Well, I don't plan to live to be twenty-five anyway, so who cares?"

While I was in Central Park, I ran into a lady I knew. She was really a sweet lady. I used to walk her dog sometimes. She took one look at me and said, "You need to go to detox." I told her I wasn't going. She told me she'd meet me there the next day and take me. She left me standing there.

At that moment something happened. Suddenly I was afraid I wasn't going to live through the night. Usually I hoped I would die—it seemed like a relief. But all of a sudden I wanted to live.

I hit my knees in the middle of Central Park and started to pray to a God I didn't know and didn't understand. I prayed, "Just keep me alive through the night."

But I kept using all night. I crashed with this guy I knew and we smoked crack all night long, running back and forth to the ATM and in and out of the bathroom. Every time I sat there in the bathroom with a needle in my arm, I was going, "God, please don't let this one take me out."

The next day I had run out of drugs so I kept my word. I had nothing but my backpack and journal. I didn't even have underwear. I went to Central Park and the lady was waiting for me. She brought me underwear—things like that touch your heart when you feel like nobody wants you.

We went to detox. This time, though, my insurance wouldn't go through. The lady put down her credit card and paid for my entire detox. If it weren't for her, I would not be alive today.

I felt like the scum of the earth walking in there. I was just grateful to take a shower and to sleep in a bed again, able to stretch out and not have to curl up on the bottom of someone else's bed, like a dog. This was as good as it could get in my mind.

I went through an awful lot of treatment. I was in a program in Manhattan that was an old-style behavioral modification place. I hated it—I honestly did. I eventually moved to another place for a full year.

About the time I got out of treatment I started thinking about acting again—something I'd forgotten about for so long. Somebody handed me a pamphlet from the Improbable Players—a professional touring company that gives performances about alcohol and other drug abuse. The shows are powerful because the actors are recovering alcoholics and addicts. The shows' scenes, created from their real-life stories, dramatize the effects of substance abuse on the family and its relation to other problems, such as HIV/AIDS and violence.

For a while I fought with myself about auditioning. I didn't want to screw up—typically beating myself up. But, something kept telling me this was different. I could get over my fears because this was doing something for somebody else. It wasn't all about me getting applause. It was helping somebody else.

I was so excited when I was called to join. We started playing scenes from our lives. One of our plays, *Passing It On,* is about HIV/AIDS and substance abuse. It focuses on making responsible choices and includes the real stories of the four actors who are in recovery, some of whom are HIV-positive. The show begins with the average teen who is "unaffected" by HIV or AIDS. The show addresses the dangers of denial and stereotyping, why choices are limited and values are compromised when someone picks up a drink or a drug, and how to talk with friends and partners about safer sex and/or abstinence.

A student wrote, after seeing the show, "I can't believe that I can get AIDS. And it feels kind of weird writing that because it's the first time I've admitted I can get it. The play was very moving and brought tears to my eyes."

It's important for me to let kids know it's OK to feel a certain way. For so long I was scared of my hurt and anger. I turned the anger inward and became depressed. Even now, for me to say "I'm pissed off" can be a challenge. But no one can tell me I have no right to feel a certain way. Everyone's perception is different, so no one can judge how I feel about something, and it's OK if they don't agree.

My shyness and low self-esteem are still with me—they're something I still struggle with. But, now I know to talk to someone who won't put me down. I journal, sit outside, pray, read anything comforting, and meditate.

I also know I can be on great terms with some sort of higher power and still be scared to death of people. I purposely go out and help somebody else because if I try to help somebody, suddenly I stop thinking about everything that's wrong with me. I start thinking about what I can do for someone else. My shyness fades into the background for a little bit.

I'm going back to school—there are 150 zillion different things I want to do. I look at the school catalog and want to take 90 percent of the classes—I remember when I couldn't be interested in anything for more than five minutes if it wasn't related to drinking or drugs.

I used drugs to escape from the reality of my life—a life filled with fear. But my choice of escape became a poison. A poison so deadly I finally was forced to choose between life and death. The day in the park, when I chose life, was the day my healing began.

Invite the Improbable Players to your school. Contact: The Improbable Players, Inc., P. O. Box 746, Watertown, Massachusetts 02272-0746. Tel: 800-437-4303. Fax: 617-926-8315. Web site: **www.players.org/players**.

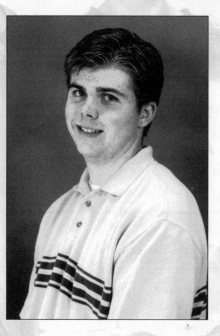

CHAPTER 7

The Fight for Life

JON BYINGTON

]F AN ADULT DESCRIBED ME, HE OR SHE WOULD SAY, "Jon is very mature for his age; he's responsible; he's dependable. He's the Eagle Scout who chairs the Eureka City Youth Council, an advisory board to the Eureka, California, City Council."

What they did not know was how depressed I was. In spring 1997, a personal problem seemed overwhelming. I can hardly describe the sadness. I stayed in my room and cried. I did that whole guy thing, thinking, "I can deal with this on my own; I don't need to share my feelings with others." I didn't talk to my family; I just cut off communication with the world. I wasn't interested in hanging out with my friends. After school I would come home, go up to my room, and sleep for hours.

Depression is described as having blinders on, where you can't see the positive things in life. Once you're depressed about something, everything else is going to make you more depressed—even things that normally wouldn't get to you. It's a downward spiral. So it wasn't surprising that suicidal thoughts crossed my mind. I just wanted to end the pain.

I needed to talk to someone and get help. But, I just couldn't—my problem was too personal to share. As hard as I tried, I couldn't make the intense pain go away. I was feeling worse each day, not better. Searching the Web I found a suicide prevention program called the Yellow Ribbon Program. I decided to e-mail them for more information.

That e-mail changed my life. The founders of the Light for Life Foundation, Dale and Dar Emme, started the Yellow Ribbon Program after their son, Michael, committed suicide. When I spoke with Dale, he told me of his son's death and how, through his program, he wanted to help other teens find a way to control their pain, not end their pain. I heard the passion in his voice when he told me about the yellow ribbon card.

The front has a yellow ribbon on it. The card reads:

THIS RIBBON IS A LIFELINE.

It carries the message that there are those who care and will help! If you are in need and don't know how to ask for help, take this card to a counselor, teacher, clergy, parent, or friend and say:

"I NEED TO USE MY YELLOW RIBBON."

The Yellow Ribbon Program is in loving memory of Michael Emme

The back of the card reads:

THIS CARD IS A CRY FOR HELP!

- *STAY with the person—you are their lifeline!*
- *LISTEN, really listen—they may not be able to tell.*
- *GET them to or call someone who can help!*

I knew our community needed the program. Dale sent me information. I read through the materials and began to plan the proposal I was going to make to the Youth Council. I began to feel better. All of the negative energy, all of the things I'd built up inside of me, seemed to be diminishing. I was making something positive out of the sadness I'd been feeling.

In September 1997 I went to the Youth Council with the idea, and they were all supportive. We decided to plan a youth suicide prevention week during February 1998.

One morning in December changed everything. I was sitting in my early morning church class that I go to before school and our teacher said, "I have some news to tell you. Last night Ricky Moses killed himself."

I just sat there in shock. It didn't really register at first. I didn't see him the day before, but everyone said he'd acted normal—just his regular self.

Ricky and I had gone to school together since elementary school. I thought about all of the different activities we had been involved in together through our church. I cried for Ricky. I wished I had known how much pain he was in. Maybe I could have helped him.

Here we were, planning the Yellow Ribbon Program for suicide prevention, and in the same week we were scheduled to meet with counselors to discuss the details, Ricky took his life.

Even though my own depression was better, Ricky's death deeply affected me. I needed to talk with someone and went to a counselor a couple of times after Ricky's suicide.

Then, with friends, I started working on the Yellow Ribbon Program as a way to fight my depression and sadness over Ricky's death. Now, unfortunately, we knew firsthand how badly our students needed this program. We needed to get the cards out as soon as possible.

A local oral surgeon who was very active in the community, Dr. Richard Rog, gave us $250 to print the first cards. We put a local crisis center number on it, and the card reads, *"in loving memory of Ricky Moses."*

At the same time the counselors changed their minds. They felt there was too much pain after Ricky's death and said that if there was going to be an assembly, it needed to be an uplifting one. At the Youth Council, we were so angry. Our friend had just killed himself, and we were told we could not help everyone else.

Since there was no way to work around policy, we made them commit to a suicide prevention week the third week in September 1998. We decided that if we had to wait, then we were going to involve every high school in our county.

And that's what we did. I sent letters to every public, private, and alternative high school. At first most school administrators said, "It hasn't happened here. There's not a problem in the community. If you start talking about suicide, it's just going to give people ideas."

Not true. If you know about depression and know someone who's been depressed, you know suicide has already crossed his or her mind. You're not going to be giving them any ideas; you're just letting them know you care about them. If they are thinking about suicide, the Yellow Ribbon card lets them know they can talk to you because you're not scared to talk about the issue.

The program became my personal mission. With good information from the program and our persistence, schools started saying yes to the week. I wrote more letters, this time to junior high schools and colleges in the area, and I faxed congresspeople for their support.

Now I just needed a way to pay for more cards, Dale and Dar's visit, and brochures. Thanks to a $3,500 grant from St. Joseph Hospital, we were able to do it all. Then right before the week began, the governor of California, Pete Wilson, proclaimed it the Yellow Ribbon Week to Prevent Youth Suicide.

Dale and Dar came to speak at each school. Dar talked about Michael and how great a kid he was—a bright, funny, loving teen who was always helping others. She spoke of how Mike cancelled his order for a new transmission for his car and bought two used ones from the salvage yard instead so that his classmate could get his car running also. Then she courageously told us Mike left a note warning them not to blame themselves and that he loved them. The note was signed, "Love, Mike 11:45 P.M." Mike shot himself in his car in the family's driveway. At 11:52 his parents pulled into the driveway—seven minutes too late.

Dale explained Mike took his life when he did not know how to let someone know he was in trouble and needed help. Dale talked about just being a friend, and if someone hands you a card, know you're a lifeline and stay with that person. Before the assembly we handed yellow ribbon cards to each student so they would not have to walk up and get one, with other people looking at them, thinking they may be suicidal or depressed. Just holding their own card and thinking about Ricky made the students see the program's value.

Usually during school assemblies the students are rowdy and you can't get them quiet. The auditorium was silent while Dale spoke. You always have lots of materials left under the seats when assemblies are over. Not one card was left behind.

Dale and Dar talked about the warning signs of suicide, like giving away possessions, abrupt changes in personality, neglect of academic work and/or personal appearance, withdrawal from people they love, and depression, among other signs. They offered coping strategies, encouraging students to be open with their feelings and not to tolerate physical, emotional, or sexual abuse from anyone but to get help immediately.

Since that week we have printed and given away about 25,000 cards. There have been three documented cases of teens taken to a mental health department twenty-four-hour crisis unit when they used their Yellow Ribbon card.

The Yellow Ribbon Program holds a special place in my heart. I still get down every once and awhile, but not like before. The program helped me work through Ricky's suicide by doing something positive for others. I now know Ricky did not die in vain.

Across the country 1,500 lives have been saved. Two million Yellow Ribbon cards have been distributed. Help save precious lives and start a Yellow Ribbon Program in your area. Contact: Yellow Ribbon Suicide Prevention Program, P. O. Box 644, Westminster, Colorado 80030-0644. Tel: 303-429-3530 Fax: 303-426-4496. Web site: **www.yellowribbon.org.** E-mail: ask4help@yellowribbon.org.

Richard Manson

Special Delivery

AVVI AGENT

December 1997

Dear Mama,

I wish I could come visit you. I don't care if the prison is hours away. I know you say you don't think it's safe for us to come because of the hate crimes happening on the back roads. But I think you really don't want us to see you living like you are. But Mama, I miss you.

Sometimes the struggle is too much. I know we had our share of problems. While you were under the influence of drugs you said and did some things that hurt me. When you couldn't pay the electric or water bill, the embarrassment of using a neighbor's toilet or studying at night by candlelight was more than a teen should have to experience. The days of not being able to buy all the things my cousins and friends had, let alone the necessary hygiene items like deodorant, toothpaste, or underclothes, were hard for me. Kids laughing at us and talking about us behind our backs really hurt.

But not having you around is worse. I've spent my high school years without you. I've celebrated too many birthdays alone. You make me want to give up on you. You make me want to give up on me. But I can't.

I think about my sisters and how they're affected by your absence. One of your daughters ran away at age sixteen. I hear she is out on the streets doing drugs, selling her body, and in and out of jail. I'm living with my sister who had a baby when she was sixteen and now can barely keep a steady job. Our relatives are talking bad about us and just waiting for me to end up in a no-win situation like my sisters.

I also think about what other people tell me: "Avvi, you are the backbone of your family. Everyone else has made mistakes; you're the only one who hasn't. You're still in school and you're working at the hospital bringing in some type of income. You're the strong one."

You know what? I choose to listen to the people who believe in me—my family at Girls Inc. Without you here to talk to, I know I can go to them for anything. I had the "mother-daughter" talks with them. I learned about sex, incest, rape, date rape, and pregnancy prevention through their programs. The instructors are always there for me whenever I need encouragement, motivation, or just a friend. They have taught me to be strong, smart, and bold.

I work hard to keep a good G.P.A. and to help out at home. I have a goal. I want to prove to people in our community and everywhere else that something good can come out of a hard situation. I don't have to come from a wealthy or happy family to succeed. I want people to say, "Hey, this girl came from the contaminated streets of peer pressure, drugs, teenage pregnancy, and crime. She could have easily joined the cycle of poverty. She could have joined a gang. But look at her—she's in college."

As a teenager going through all of this—not having you around and not having a well-kept house like my friends—it's tough. But I remain strong. I only have one request from you.

You have to change. I want you to come home a new you. You've missed too much of my life. I really need you here for me. You owe me something. I love you, Mama.

Love,
Your baby, Avvi

I wrote that letter to my mother when I was fifteen years old. She wrote me back. She let me know she had started a group session at the prison. It was made up of women she was incarcerated with—women who used to hate each other. She wrote me that she told them that before she was in prison she was out in the world strung out on drugs and headed toward a dead end. She went on to tell them all about me and how I was trying to make something of myself. She told her group she owed me something. She told them she was going to change, not only for herself, but for me, too.

I could barely finish reading the letter I was crying so much. I hoped and prayed she would stay strong.

Mama was finally released in January 1998. She's not on drugs, and soon she'll celebrate her fifth year clean. She and I spend a lot of time together. She loves going to church and spending time with her grandbabies and the rest of her family. Every other Sunday she and I cook for some of the disadvantaged people in our neighborhood. We'll go there and barbecue, sing gospel, and pray.

On behalf of Girls Inc., I go out and tell my story, letting people know you can be anything you want to be. Once I even found myself talking to a young girl who was standing at a bus stop with a baby in a stroller, one in her arms, and one on the way. I told her what I went through to get where I am now. I passed on to her the lesson I learned so well—the message Girls Inc. taught me: "It doesn't matter where you come from, as long as you know where you're going."

Girls ages six to eighteen years can take charge of their lives and overcome barriers they face. Girls Inc. helps prepare today's girls for tomorrow's world. Contact: Girls Inc., 2040 Empire Central Drive, Dallas Texas 75235. Tel: 214-654-4536. Fax: 214-350-8115. Web site: **www.girlsinc.org**.

CHAPTER 9

Sgt. Pepper's Photography 1999

Building Bridges

CHARLIE SIMMONS

T
HE DAY STARTED OUT JUST LIKE MOST OTHER TUESDAYS. I'm in a show choir called "Unclaimed Freight" at Columbine High School; we rehearse in the mornings before school. I got to school at 6:50 A.M., saw friends, and said hello on my way in.

We went through the day normally until fifth period, which for me is concert choir. We were starting our warm-ups when a student in the choir came into the room and said there was a guy downstairs with a gun.

This student was known to be a jokester. But he had a pretty serious look on his face and I saw kids running by when I looked out the window. The choir director told us all to chill out. He didn't want us to panic—there were 114 choir members. He was walking toward the door near the stairwell when two girls opened the door and we heard two shotgun bursts. Half the choir hit the ground.

My first instinct was to run. I went out the opposite door that the two girls had come in, into a corridor that leads to the auditorium.

I saw a stampede of people running down the hallways. I heard screams. I decided I wasn't going to try and join the mob, so I ran into the auditorium. I stood at the back of the auditorium, wondering what refuge kids were finding behind plastic chairs. Then I heard the semi-automatic fire. At some point, somebody pulled the fire alarm down, so lots of kids in the east end of the school got out without a notion of what was happening.

I headed out the north door. I saw the fire doors at the north hallway—the main hallway—were closed, so I turned and ran for the front door. As I got closer I saw there were already bullet holes in the glass.

Seeing the bullet holes made me run even faster. I reached the front door and pushed it open. The bullets had weakened the glass, and shattered glass came showering out of the door all over me. I just kept running. I didn't even notice the blood all over me until much later. I later went to the hospital for stitches.

About fifteen kids followed me and got out the front door. I learned later that we barely made it out. Seconds later one of the shooters, Dylan, came into the main office and started spraying bullets.

I saw a friend, and we ran to her house. From her house we could see the front of the school. We watched the police, the firemen, the paramedics, the SWAT teams from Denver and other areas, and the National Guard as they showed up. State patrolmen and sheriffs pulled up and got out of their cars with their guns. They stood behind trees and told kids to run.

The next few hours seemed to last forever. At first I thought a kid was in the school with a gun and that he may have shot a few kids, maybe injuring some-body, but I hoped he hadn't caused much harm. As I watched the different teams of police show up and heard on the radio there were two gunmen, possibly three, I started to realize how big this really was.

A group of police drove a fire truck close to the building. They jumped out and ran inside. I found out later that lots of those guys weren't trained to be in the positions they were leading. They went in and risked their lives—they didn't even think about it, they just did it to save lives.

It scared me to death when later reports on the radio said that twenty-five kids were killed. I hadn't seen my best friend, Dustin, come out. I prayed he was all right. I didn't find out he was safe until much later. He had hidden in a bathroom in the kitchen and was evacuated with other kids who hid nearby.

It was a living nightmare. It was a bad day multiplied by the biggest number you can think of. The day seemed to go on for years—hours were days; everything was wrong.

The night of the shootings a lot of us went to a service at St. Francis Cabrini Catholic Church. It was really emotional for all of us because we knew our friends who should be there were gone forever. I couldn't even imagine that friends of mine—Cory, Rachel, Isaiah, Cassie—wouldn't be back at school. How could their lives end so violently? How could Eric's and Dylan's minds get so messed up?

For the longest time I didn't know what day it was, the day of the week, the date—it all just kind of ran together. I didn't eat anything for three days—I had a sick feeling inside. I kept crying. Every emotion ran through my head. I was sad, mad, confused, helpless, and lost.

I spent a little time with my parents. I hugged them a lot and told them I loved them. But I needed to be with my friends, the people who had experienced this with me. People can say, "I know how you feel," but it's not true if you weren't there.

There were lots of counselors around. Media were everywhere. People showed up trying to get kids to come to their church. What touched me most were the people who came just to be available for us. They were there if we needed someone to talk to. They didn't force themselves on us at all.

We had lots of get-togethers on private property where the media couldn't get to us. We would just go and be together—the first week that's all we did. We didn't have to speak to each other—it was enough to share the silence with each other.

The first place that the faculty and students got back together was at a community church. The student body was sitting together waiting for the faculty. The choir decided we wanted to sing because before the tragedy we were practicing some very spiritual, very touching songs that had a high level of difficulty. We got up together and went up on the stage. The faculty still hadn't made it in, so I was "volunteered" to conduct.

We started singing "Ave Maria." I had chills and the hair on the back of my neck was standing up. We hadn't warmed up and the song has some very high notes for females. But they were just ripping them out—the sound was unbelievable.

As we sang "The Lord's Prayer," the faculty came into the sanctuary and started singing with us. Then the whole student body joined in. Here we were, together for the first time after a living nightmare, singing "The Lord's Prayer." As I conducted and heard the most beautiful sounds ever, I felt the love in that room. At that moment I knew we would all be all right.

About a week later, a woman from a Jefferson community group came up to me at church and asked me if I would be willing to give my input about getting some sort of youth center going. I agreed to help.

The idea was to get a safe place where kids could be with each other and not have to worry about not being accepted. We wanted teens to have a free gathering place to communicate and find support in communication with others. We wanted an environment that promoted conversation, outreach, counseling, and healing in the Littleton, Colorado, area.

We started throwing out names for the group, anything we could come up with. Somebody threw out the name S.H.O.U.T.S. We all liked it and voted it to be the official name.

I thought it would be cool if it was an acronym, so I started working with words. We finally came up with Students Helping Others Unite Together Socially.

The Jefferson Mental Health Center found a space—the top floor of the Ascot Theatre in Littleton—and thought it would work well. We looked at it and really liked it. They set up a one-year lease with the possibility of extensions.

We placed an ad in the paper for young adult mentors. The ad said we were looking for "cool adults." As we interviewed the applicants we looked for people who were very friendly to teens. We selected one male and one female, so that if a female student didn't feel comfortable talking to a guy, she had a woman to talk to, and a guy student had a male to talk to if he wanted to.

The two mentors we chose are great people who have worked with teens before. They aren't strict. They're there just to supervise, to make sure nothing goes wrong, and to make sure everyone is treated with respect. They're close to our age, so they're friends for us to talk to. They fit right in.

S.H.O.U.T.S. is a great hangout. We have pool, ping-pong, foosball, and air hockey. We've got painting supplies if kids want to work on art projects. A big screen TV and VCR were donated so we can watch movies. We have a digital music system with a keyboard plugged into a computer for kids who want to create their own music, record it, and take it with them. Counselors are available if anyone needs to talk with a professional. We're open Sundays from 7 P.M. until 10 P.M. and Mondays through Wednesdays from 3 P.M. until 10 P.M. We close early enough so we can get home before curfew.

Creating S.H.O.U.T.S. has helped me move forward. Having a positive focus took my mind off the tragedy. I could deal with it more easily knowing I was doing something to help others.

Going back into the school before they started tearing everything out and remodeling also helped me. After seeing the damage and hearing detailed descriptions of everything, I thanked God that Eric and Dylan didn't accomplish even part of their goal. If the two propane bombs in the cafeteria had gone off, we would have lost 800 people, not fifteen.

I went to the places where my friends took their final breaths. I said silent prayers and my last good-byes. It was closure on their lives for me.

My friend Dustin and I spoke to a group of kids in Alabama about the shootings. I asked them to raise their hands if they had a secret that their parents didn't know about them. There was not a single kid who didn't raise his or her hand. I told them that with teenagers, there's always something you want to keep from your parents. But find somebody that you feel comfortable around and talk to them about your secret. Talking is the key.

Eric and Dylan had a secret and told no one. Maybe nobody let them know they had somebody to talk to if they needed to. I think they were angry at the world. I think they had problems with themselves or with their families or with others they just couldn't work out. I think that someone wasn't around to touch Eric or Dylan's lives.

I recently heard an awesome quote: "You can build walls and you can build bridges with the same material." Why put up a wall when you can just accept each other as equals?

There's no reason in the world not to like somebody. Sure, you can get upset with someone, but that's no reason for hatred. We're all the same—we all have hearts and lungs and brains. We breathe the same air and live together on this planet. We need to live together as one. I hope that people can find it in their hearts to accept one another.

April 20, 2000, is going to be very hard. I'm hoping we'll be able to look back at April 20, 1999, and see the good we've created from the worst experience of our lives. We know there are problems in our society. Here in the Columbine community, we're looking at them, seeing them, fixing them. We're tearing down the walls and building strong bridges.

Would you like your school to have an innovative program like S.H.O.U.T.S.? Contact: S.H.O.U.T.S., Ascot Theater, 9136 West Bowles Avenue, Littleton, Colorado 80123. Tel: 303-972-7977.

Join the worldwide effort to promote nonviolence. Students in schools all over the world are signing the "I Will" pledge:

As a part of the _____Community, I WILL . . .

- I will pledge to be a part of the solution.
- I will eliminate taunting from my own behavior.
- I will encourage others to do the same.
- I will do my part to make _____ a safe place by being more sensitive to others.
- I will set the example of a caring individual.
- I will eliminate profanity towards others from my language.
- I will not let my words or actions hurt others . . . and if others won't become a part of the solution, I WILL.

Signing here reflects your commitment to your pledge through graduation 2000. The pledge is printed in five languages. Make the call and have free materials sent to you for your school. Contact: Hillsboro High School, 3812 Hillsboro Pike, Nashville, Tennessee 37215. Tel: 615-298-8400. Fax: 615-298-8402. E-mail: lheron@educator.mci.net. Web site: **www.iwillpledge.nashville.com**.

_____

Prestige by Lifetouch 1999

Born to Win

JAKE REPP

THE DOCTOR CALLED MY MOM AND DAD AND ME INTO HIS OFFICE. He said, "Jake, you have angiosarcoma, a very rare form of cancer. You have thirty tumors in your foot. In the last fifteen years there have only been a few instances in the United States in which this form of cancer occurred only in an extremity. It usually is found in the internal organs, but for some reason yours started at your foot and spread to your ankle."

How could this be? During a basketball game—a summer league—I had come down wrong on my ankle. After limping around all month, I decided to get it checked out. School was starting, and I needed to be in top condition for basketball season. I thought at worst that I had fractured my ankle.

The doctor continued, "You really don't have a choice here. The biggest problem with this type of cancer is there is no cure. Chemo and radiation won't work. We need to perform a below-the-knee amputation."

I remember going home and going to my room. I had a really, really good cry. I thought, "Why me? I'm only sixteen years old. I'm a good kid; I haven't done anything wrong in my life."

That afternoon was the only time I felt sorry for myself. I thought about my grandmother, Baba—she had passed away a couple of years before—and how brave she was. She had diabetes. Because of complications, her leg was amputated. No matter how sick Baba felt, she always smiled and never complained.

I talked to God for a while that day. I said, "I'll try to be as strong as Baba was. If this means giving part of my right leg so I can keep my life, then I'm completely game, because I'm not about to lose my life."

The morning of the surgery I listened to a song from my favorite group, the Beastie Boys. It really gave me a push because the lyrics say, "Just do it, do it, put your mind to it and do it." I told myself to be strong, to just get it over with.

The first few days after the surgery were the hardest. I experienced phantom pains. Those really hurt. The brain doesn't understand at first that a body part is gone. I would wake up in the middle of the night having to scratch my toe and I couldn't. This would go on for three hours—it was torture.

I was up on crutches right away. The next step was to get my prosthesis—an artificial leg. I'll never forget that day. The physical therapist told me walking with my prosthesis would be a difficult thing. I should expect it to take one and a half to two months to learn to walk without crutches. I looked at him and said, "You know what? I'm going to learn to walk without crutches in two weeks."

It ended up that I was half a week off. When I walked into the therapy clinic, my therapist held up a basketball. He said, "Here, Jake, since you proved to me you could walk in record time, let's shoot around."

I slowly walked outside to the court. I stood at the free throw line, and he threw me the basketball. I threw it up and sunk it. You can't imagine the feeling when I heard the *swoosh*. I thought, "I've still got it. I'm still the same person."

From then on, my progress just took off. A month later I learned how to jog. I was already playing basketball again, and during my free period at lunch, I was shooting baskets with my friends.

My dad took me to San Antonio to meet Thomas Bourgeois, the Number 1 pentathlete in the United States. A pentathlete is an athlete participating in five events in the Paralympics. The Paralympics are elite sport events for athletes from six different disability groups. They emphasize, however, the participants' athletic achievements rather than their disabilities. The Paralympic Games have always been held in the same year as the Olympic Games. In Atlanta in 1996, 3,195 athletes participated. More than 4,000 athletes will participate in the Sydney Paralympic games in 2000.

Thomas won a Bronze Medal in '92 in Barcelona and a Silver Medal in Atlanta in '96. When we met up with him, I couldn't help but stare.

Here was this professional athlete wearing shorts exposing his prosthetic—a black, robotic looking device—and looking totally confident. He even had a sandal on his foot. And here I was wearing long pants trying my best to hide my leg.

After lunch we went to the basketball courts. He and I played three college kids and beat them. I couldn't believe his moves. He made those guys look like little kids.

Thomas said, "Jake, it's unbelievable that, in six months, you are playing ball like this. You have a future in athletics." I went with Thomas to the Summer Nationals to watch him compete. To see all those athletes with prosthetics was mind-boggling.

I ended up taking a clinic with Dennis Oehler, a Gold Medal winner in the '88 Paralympics. He puts on clinics for new amputees and teaches them how to run again. We started with a fast walk and then a jog. He told me to sprint like I normally would. I took off running. It was nine months after my leg was amputated and I was sprinting. Tears filled my eyes—I felt like I was flying.

Dennis told me he had never seen anyone run so soon after an amputation. He entered me in the amateur 100-meter race. I ran a 15-second hundred, which is pretty bad. But I finished the race and I felt incredible.

I came home and told my parents I wanted to start running—but a sprinting prosthesis costs $20,000. Luckily, Nova Care, the manufacturer, was so amazed with my progress that they sent me a leg for free.

I trained for the Nationals. I wasn't ready to compete with my old school team, but I got to train with them.

The Nationals in Fairfax, Virginia, were awesome. This time I ran a 13.5-second hundred, qualifying me for the World Championships!

I went to the Olympic Training Center in Chula Vista, California. Only U.S. Olympic and Paralympic athletes can train there. I worked really hard knowing I only had two weeks to get ready.

The World Championships were held in Birmingham, England. There were 1,600 athletes from more than sixty countries. My parents and sister came to see me compete for the first time.

In the prelim I ran the hundred in 12.8 seconds. The next day we ran the quarter finals—I ran a 12.75, qualifying me for the semifinals, but there I got totally blown away.

I was just happy I was even there in the first place, with people who shared my philosophy. The feeling—the spirit—it's all about athletes from all over the world overcoming adversity and giving everything we have.

When I got back home, I tried out for the track team at my school and made the varsity squad. I think I'm one of the first amputees to ever run varsity track against non-amputees.

At the first race, as I lined up against two-legged strangers, I felt I had to break the ice. My dad told me, from the beginning, that people were going to act the way I act. He said to go into every situation with a positive attitude.

I looked at the other guys in my heat and said, "Am I at the wrong meet? I thought I was supposed to be at a disabled meet. You guys are going to kill me."

One guy said, "I've seen you in the newspaper. You're supposed to be fast. We heard about you. You can't pull that on us."

I thought if I could beat just one of them, I'd be happy. I ended up finishing fourth and beating three or four guys. They told me I was the fastest one-legged guy they'd ever seen. During the season I ran a consistent 11.55.

My goal is to compete in the Paralympics this year. In the meantime, I train hard. I also go to Scottish Rite Hospital and hang out with little kids. It's the greatest when I see a little guy, five years old, with his prosthesis, and I can lift up my pant leg and say, "Oh, look, I've got one, too!"

Recently a guy from Colorado called me. He read about me in a disabled magazine. He lost his leg in a car accident and needed to talk to someone. We talked about everything—how to take a shower, how to treat the stump, how important it is to be positive. He calls me whenever he wants to talk.

I was one of the lucky ones. My parents, coaches, and friends supported me from the moment I was diagnosed. I met Thomas, who believed in me, and then Dennis, who taught me how to run. I'm going to see where my running takes me, but when that's over, I'd love to do what Dennis does—go out and teach young amputees how to run again. I also want to continue to tell my story to kids and adults who are suffering—anyone who's lost faith and thinks life is over—that if you look for something good to come from something bad, you'll find it every time. With the right attitude, you always win.

For more information on all of the summer and winter sports available for physically challenged athletes, contact: Disabled Sports USA, 451 Hungerford Drive, Suite 100, Rockville, Maryland 20850. Web site: **www.dsusa.org**.

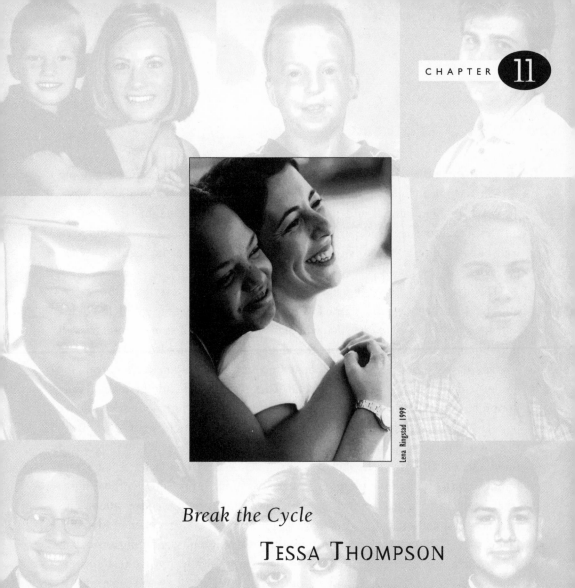

CHAPTER 11

Lena Ringstad 1999

Break the Cycle

TESSA THOMPSON

]STARTED A RELATIONSHIP WHEN] WAS IN THE NINTH GRADE, when I was just beginning Santa Monica High School. It was a transition point for me in a lot of ways, going to high school and then meeting this guy I thought was wonderful. Jeff made me feel special from the beginning. He was a senior and very well liked—I didn't have to worry about meeting people or not getting invited places.

The first thing I did when we started going out was cut myself off from everyone else. I isolated myself, because I wanted to spend all my time with Jeff. I didn't join any after-school activities; that would take away from the time I could be with him. I didn't spend time with other friends—Jeff was all I needed.

One day a group of young women from an organization called Break the Cycle™ came to speak to my health class. This group is the nation's first and only nonprofit organization to take a proactive approach to ending domestic violence by focusing specifically on young people ages twelve through twenty-two. Break the Cycle™ presents a three-day, interactive education and prevention program in middle school and high school classrooms, juvenile detention facilities, and community youth groups throughout Los Angeles County. It provides youth with free legal counsel and representation, including restraining and protective orders, support services, and referral assistance. The founder, an attorney named Meredith Blake, spoke about abusive relationships—the warning signs, anything as small as a possessive relationship to anything as big as a physically abusive relationship, where you need to get a restraining order.

They involved us in mock trials—for example, what it would feel and look like if a teen had to get a restraining order. For me, I was playing a part. I had not even known that a teen could get a restraining order. It just seemed like these were things that happened to other people, not me, and I would never have to be concerned with a restraining order, or for that matter, an abusive relationship.

We were given handouts and a Break the Cycle™ business card. The front of the card has the nonprofit's contact information while the back of the card reads:

You have a right to a safe and healthy relationship free from violence and free from fear. Know the warning signs of an abusive relationship:

- Continuous Criticism
- Controlling or Dominant Behavior
- Extreme Jealousy or Insecurity
- Explosive Temper
- Isolating You from Family and Friends
- History of Verbal Threats
- Preventing You From Doing What You Want to Do
- History of Violence
- Big Mood Swings
- Making False Accusations
- Possessiveness
- Financial Control
- Telling You What to Do

I took all of the information for a friend who I felt was in an abusive relationship. But it did flash through my mind that Jeff was jealous and very possessive. I laughed to myself, thinking I was being ridiculous—I should be glad Jeff loved me and cared about me. I ended up putting all of the information away, not even giving it to my friend.

I did share the information with Jeff, though, and we joked about it together. I said teasingly, "Well, you are possessive," and he said, "Well, you're always jealous." We were not serious at all, yet deep down I wanted him to know those qualities bugged me.

Then I wondered whether Jeff's controlling behavior should bother me at all.

This was my first relationship. Maybe this was what an intense, passionate relationship was all about.

We kept going out, even though Jeff was becoming more and more controlling. If another guy talked to me, Jeff would flip out. If I wore something he did not deem "appropriate," he'd get really upset. He'd embarrass me, yelling at me in front of other kids.

I guess at first I was flattered that he loved me so much—enough to want me to not look too good for other guys and not to wear clothes that showed off my body too much. But the tedium of having to constantly "be on guard" talking to a guy, even if he was just a friend, and having to watch what I wore began to feel really wrong.

When Jeff became upset we'd have a two-hour argument about the problem—every single time. When the women from Break the Cycle™ visited, they had showed us a circle graph that states, "Tension builds, tension breaks, it explodes, and then everything is better." At the time, I remember thinking that a graph can't possibly describe a relationship. Feelings and emotions can't be shown on a graph.

But that graph perfectly describes the cycle we went through time after time—the circumstances were just different each time. Tension built, he'd explode, and then I'd always think that Jeff was my dream boyfriend again, because we'd work everything out. We'd enter the honeymoon stage after an argument; he would be gentle and caring—like something you would see in the movies. I would think, "OK, he's really changed this time. Everything is going to be better." I really wanted to believe that. I loved him. I wanted to invest my trust in him, in the hope that he would change.

For two years I went through this cycle. By then I wanted to be with other people, but I couldn't be. Jeff wanted me to spend all of my time with him. He would never say I couldn't go to a mall or to a movie with other girls. Instead, he'd tell me I shouldn't trust girls. When I'd ask him why not, he'd say, "You just can't. Don't you trust me?" Then I'd feel wrong questioning him, and I wouldn't go out with my friends, thinking he was probably right.

As time went by, I became an emotional mess. I couldn't focus on homework or my family, and nothing was important to me anymore.

The situation was ironic. Jeff and I looked like the perfect couple. Everyone wrote comments in my yearbook like, "I hope you and Jeff stay together forever." We were known as a couple—my identity was that I was Jeff's girlfriend. I had no friends and I had given up my close relationship with my family. I had totally given myself away to Jeff.

I couldn't tell my mom the truth. I was ashamed for her to know; I didn't want her to think badly of me. My family thought he was the perfect guy. And I was close with his family. Knowing I needed to speak with someone who could be objective, I went to Break the Cycle™. I pretended I was there for a friend, but every question I asked was really for me.

I learned a lot that day. Meredith discussed abusive behavior with me. I thought about the fact that Jeff would fight with another guy if he looked at him the wrong way. I began to realize that he was fighting over the smallest things, and the next physical fight could be with me.

Some time later I heard a psychologist say that guys who punch walls will, at some point, have a problem deciphering between a wall and a face. All they know is that they feel better afterward.

I had tried nine times to break up with Jeff, but I always gave in to him. This time I had the support of Meredith and Break the Cycle™. I was ready to end this craziness.

For the tenth time, I broke up with Jeff, even though he cried, begged, and promised things would change. I stood strong this time. When he told me I was nothing without him—that I didn't have any other friends, that I wasn't involved in any outside activities, that I had nobody but him who cared about me, and I needed him—I chose not to listen this time.

It was the most weird, awkward, uncomfortable feeling ending the relationship. I had gotten into a serious relationship and had put my own personal growth on hold. All I did was give and give more to Jeff. I gave myself away for two years. Now I was alone without a clue about who I was.

But Jeff did not take my identity from me. I gave it to him. It's hard for me when people make our relationship a "him" issue, because this was not about him. I'll be the first to admit that I was manipulated into a lot of things, but even so, I gave those things away.

Why don't guys have the proper resources or tools to have healthy relationships? What have they learned from their parents? What haven't they learned? Why are girls so quick to give so much of themselves away for a guy? It's pretty frightening to know, according to statistics, that one in every four teenage relationships will become abusive.

I knew I needed to get involved in school activities right away and find out what I liked to do. I tried out for the cheerleading squad and made it! The timing was divine—it provided a vehicle for me to get to know other kids. Soon I was also involved in the drama department, making friends and realizing I never needed Jeff for my happiness—he needed me to feed his insecurities.

Our school had a week devoted to nonviolence. I asked Break the Cycle™ to come and speak about domestic violence and answer any questions. I did not intend on speaking—I was just helping organize the assembly. Other girls were writing their personal stories and having them read by someone else, following the counselors' suggestion—they were concerned for the girls' safety if their boyfriends were at the school.

The day of the assembly no one brought their stories. I guess they were afraid to share their experiences. So, after Break the Cycle™ spoke, I ended up telling my own story to the entire student assembly. Jeff had graduated, so I felt safe. I told myself I could do this; I walked up to the stage and started talking.

Wow! What a great day—I was finally free after telling the truth about our relationship. This was the first time I had ever told anyone besides Meredith. And, I had used my story to reach out to others in abusive situations.

Halfway through the assembly, a guy who had helped organize the assembly with me decided to get up and speak as well. He had watched his father physically abuse his mother, and then his father had abused him. He had never told anyone.

It was a heavy assembly, but kids told me later that it was one of the best our school had ever held.

Once I began telling my story, I felt like a terrible burden was lifted off me. Turning a very shameful, hurtful, and dark issue into educational awareness helped me begin to heal.

Recently, Meredith and I were on *Oprah!* discussing dating violence. One of my biggest reasons for going on *Oprah!* was to enlighten girls my age and anyone and everyone to this issue. Some people think that if it's not a physically abusive relationship, then it can't be that bad. I hope people will begin to understand that emotional and verbal abuse leave scars too—scars that will never go away.

Since the show has aired, women of all ages and from many different backgrounds have come up to me randomly and told me their stories. One older woman told me how much the show helped her understand her own situation.

Meredith and Break the Cycle™ gave me the courage and knowledge to leave Jeff. As busy as I am at school, I have partnered with Break the Cycle™ to help reach as many teens as possible, letting them know about abusive relationships— the signs and how to get help. I want others to know that they, too, can

successfully break the cycle and discover that the courage to give is the fuel to
live!

> If you or someone you know is in an abusive relationship, contact: Break the
> Cycle™, P. O. Box 1797, Santa Monica, California 90406-1797. Tel: 888-988-
> TEEN. Fax: 310-319-1340. E-mail: btc@pacificnet.net.
>
> Another resource for dating violence is the Abuse Prevention Services of the
> Canadian Red Cross. Contact: Canadian Red Cross, National Office, 1430
> Blair Place, 3rd Floor, Gloucester, Ontario K1J 9N2.

My Voice

BRANDON FERNANDEZ

WHEN I WAS IN FIFTH GRADE, I WENT UP TO MY TEACHER to get help with our assignment. I tried to ask the question, but I started to stutter and couldn't stop. My teacher, who supposedly had a degree in speech pathology, yelled at me. He thought yelling at me would make me stop stuttering.

Yelling at me made it worse. I went home crying.

I've always stuttered, and most teachers have never understood. I wasn't involved in many after-school activities because I was afraid I might have to speak. In school or at home with guests, I never spoke. I remember my mom's friends coming over and remarking, "Oh, he's so quiet, so well behaved." They didn't know it was because I was afraid to talk in front of people.

In the third grade there was a teacher, Mrs. Rosenberg, who used to come to our class once a week, to teach us poetry. I really got into it and started writing a lot. Mrs. Rosenberg told me she loved my work and encouraged me to write more.

She was my teacher for two years. She truly changed how I felt about myself. She was the first teacher who saw me as more than a boy who stutters.

I wrote about trees and then about my grandfather who had died about six months before. I was really attached to my grandfather, and poetry became a way for me to tell other people about him, and for me to express myself.

I continued with my poetry and writing. In sixth grade I took a photography class and discovered yet another beautiful way to express myself without speaking. I placed a 5 x 8 photo on an 8 x 10 mat and wrote a poem about the picture around the mat.

My best friend since kindergarten, Alissa, loved my art. But she also kept telling me to speak up and not to be quiet. If Alissa sees anything wrong, she'll speak out. Just from hanging out with her and being her friend, I got the courage to give it a try.

In seventh grade I raised my hand in class for the first time in years—in a class with a very supportive teacher. I started to stutter. I stopped, took a breath, and tried again. I was stuck on a simple sound and kept repeating it. I just stopped and took another breath trying to pass that simple sound and continue on. It took ten minutes to get my question out. My teacher never interrupted me. Not one kid in the class laughed or made a sound.

I learned a very important lesson that day. My friend Alissa had encouraged me to speak out. Even though I had found new ways to express myself, she didn't want me to hide behind them. She didn't want me to keep my pain inside of me. With her support, I spoke out and discovered how good I felt afterward. By facing my biggest fear—speaking in public—I let go of a lot of pain that I had held inside for many years.

Three years ago I made my confirmation. One of the nuns asked me to make a speech at the church in front of more than 1,000 people. I accepted.

I went through the whole speech without one stutter. I went home and cried afterward, I was so happy.

My writing and photography continued to improve as my confidence in myself grew. I knew I wanted to use my talents when I graduated. One day in school I read an announcement about an upcoming meeting with a group called Youth Venture. All those interested in creating new businesses were encouraged to attend.

I really had no idea what I wanted to do, but I went to hear about Youth Venture. The spokesperson told us every young person who has a creative idea about how they can make a difference in their community might become a Youth

Venturer. Youth Venture challenges and ultimately changes the belief that "kids can't" by showing the world that "kids can" and do make a difference with every venture they launch. Youth Venturers serve as role models for other young people and adults in the community, eventually "tipping" the community to recognize and encourage youth entrepreneurs as capable, significant contributors to society.

As I listened, an incredible idea came into my head. After the meeting I hurried home, wrote a proposal, and put a budget together. I turned it into Youth Venture. They gave me the grant, and E.X.P.R.E.S.S.I.O.N.S. was born.

E.X.P.R.E.S.S.I.O.N.S teaches younger children how to express themselves through poetry and photography. Classes are free—the grant pays for supplies and advertising.

The kids write their own poetry and learn about poets like Alfred Lord Tennyson, who wrote about himself and his family and friends. I emphasize the importance of expressing personal feelings.

The classes are held at the public library in Park Slope, Brooklyn. My youngest student is five and my oldest is fifteen. Parents who stay with their children start writing too, and I think that's really cool.

My friend Alissa helps me out. The neighborhood is mainly Hispanic, and she speaks Spanish well. I encourage the kids to write in Spanish, because it does help sometimes to write in the language that's most comfortable. I plan to exhibit their works at library showings and sidewalk sales.

I want to share with the children what I learned—we never have to hold our feelings inside. Whether we express ourselves through speech, poetry, or photography, every one of us has a voice with something of value to say. Now, we can be heard.

Change the role of youth in society. Take responsibility for yourself and your community by creating an organization that benefits others. Contact: Youth Venture, 1700 North Moore Street, Suite 1920, Arlington, Virginia 22209. Tel: 703-527-8300 ext. 24. Fax: 703-527-8383. E-mail: Yventure@aol.com. Web site: **www.youthventure.org**.

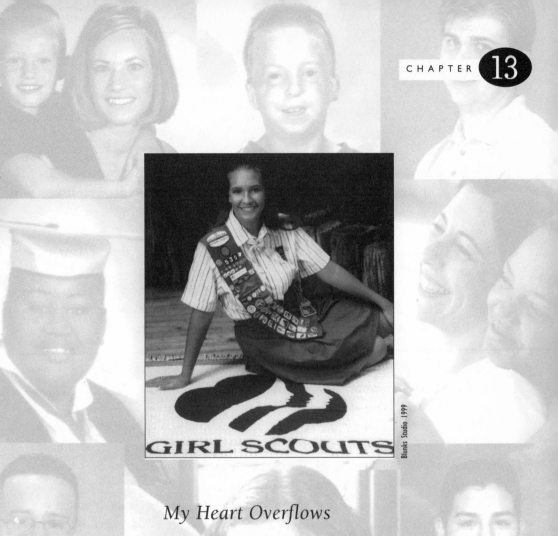

CHAPTER 13

Blunks Studio 1999

GIRL SCOUTS

My Heart Overflows

MELISSA CHAPPELL

WHEN I WAS SIX MONTHS OLD, THE DOCTORS FOUND SOMETHING wrong with my heart. They thought I had a bubble on my heart. When you have a bubble on your heart, it pops and sometimes you die. The doctors prepared my parents for the worst.

As I got older and the doctors performed an ultrasound, they discovered instead that I had a hole in my heart. It's called a VSD heart murmur.

A cardiologist in Grand Forks, North Dakota, examined me when I was ten years old. She told us she could do surgery, but she didn't feel it was necessary. She said that in a study of a hundred kids, fifty had surgery and fifty didn't. All grew up healthy and fine.

My parents decided against the surgery. The doctors told me I shouldn't be as active as a normal, healthy child would be, because physical activity is strenuous on the heart. They advised me against participating in sports.

As I got older I wanted to play softball, but my mom was leery about letting me do it. Not only do I have a hole in my heart, but I also have severe asthma. I have a breathing machine, seven inhalers, and loads of medication. So I had to work hard to convince my mom to let me play.

Finally, she decided if that's what I wanted to do, then she would let me play. So I played softball and loved it. Even when I had trouble breathing and needed medication I felt better than not playing at all.

Early on, my mom understood me. I wasn't going to avoid activities because I *may* get sick or I *may* get worse. If there's something I wanted to do and I loved it so much, I wasn't going to stay away from it.

I truly believe my positive attitude and my ability not to give in to the fears—I could be afraid to even walk outside given the doctor's warnings—has enabled me to accomplish all that I have.

Instead of worrying if I could breathe if I were outside participating actively in a sport, I made sure I had something to participate in. My father retired a couple of years ago, but throughout my childhood he was in the Air Force, which means we moved many times—New York, Mississippi, Arkansas, North Dakota, Guam, and now Oklahoma. Joining Girl Scouts—becoming part of a group of girls with goals similar to my own—helped me make new friends in each city.

I first joined the Girl Scouts in Arkansas. When we moved to Guam, there wasn't a Cadet group, so my mom and I started one. We started with three girls and ended with fifteen. Our troop was very active, earning a patch every month for tasks completed—community service projects, babysitting, CPR.

So between Girl Scouts and attending schools on the base in every city, making friends wasn't too difficult. All of us were the same—we understood the life of the Air Force child, the coming and the going we all experienced.

The Oklahoma move was different. Before I had always gone to schools on the base with other Air Force kids. Now, at fifteen years old, I was entering a new school, a school not located on a base, and I was confronted with kids who were friends since kindergarten. Their social groups were formed years before and becoming a part of one was close to impossible.

To make matters worse, there was no Girl Scout troop at the school. Before, in other new cities, scouting really helped me adjust. As important to me as the work I did in scouting was the opportunity I had to make friends in different cities through scouting.

Just as my health wasn't going to get me down, neither was this situation. I never felt sorry for myself before. I wasn't going to start now.

I found out there was a Cadet troop in Oklahoma City made up of girls from different junior highs. I immediately joined. The girls in the troop were friendly, fun, and committed to the principles of Girl Scouts. Even though we weren't in school together, I once again had a group of girls who became my good friends—girls I could depend on.

This particular troop enjoyed camping out. I had never camped out before. It was wintertime when we went. It was too cold for me because we had just moved from Guam. The sudden change of temperature made it difficult for me to breathe. I took the strongest medicine I had, and it finally kicked in. Suddenly, my breathing difficulty didn't matter. It began to snow, and I was in awe. Coming from Guam—a place that doesn't know what snow is—made the experience even more magical.

Every aspect of scouting in Oklahoma proved to be better than I could ever have hoped for. Our troop leader was great. She encouraged us to participate in scouting on a national level. She told us about a program called Wider Opportunities for Women—an annual program you have to apply for and be accepted to. She gave us a book describing the different programs.

That year I was accepted to go to Connecticut to the American Indian Scouting Association to learn about different Indian heritages. I loved it so much. Oklahoma is home to many Native Americans. After learning about different cultures I brought my new knowledge back to my council. We all gained an appreciation and respect for our Native American friends from school.

This past year I applied to the New York Wider Opportunities program called Women Then, Now and Always. Only seventy-five Girl Scouts from twenty-eight states were accepted, and I was one of them!

One of the nights we were to have dinner with Dianne Roffe-Steinrotter—the women's downhill Olympian gold medal winner. I didn't get to attend because I had to go to the doctor.

I was sorry I missed the opportunity to hear Dianne, but I was able to participate in Celebration '98, the main event. Fourteen thousand people came to hear keynote speaker Hillary Clinton urge women to celebrate how far we had come in 150 years, and to continue to fight for our rights.

We were so excited and nervous anticipating the big event. All seventy-five of us wore our Girl Scout uniforms. We carried the original Women's Rights movements flags in the opening ceremony. I proudly carried the flag before all of those people, before endless TV crews, before the Honorary President of the Girl Scouts—First Lady Hillary Clinton.

I couldn't believe I was actually a part of such an amazing moment. I couldn't believe how far Girl Scouts had taken me—from friendships to understanding the importance of women having the opportunity to make a difference in the world.

The next day I ended up in the hospital. Bug spray had been sprayed near me, and I had a really bad asthma attack. On my way to the emergency room I was wishing I could go somewhere just once without having an attack. But I also knew I was not going to let it ruin a fabulous trip.

I came back to Oklahoma appreciating Girl Scouts more than ever—if that was possible. I wished more girls knew how wonderful it was. Recently I got accepted for a job with AmeriCorps, allowing me to start scouting troops in high-risk areas while giving me a stipend and a college scholarship. This particular AmeriCorps job partners with America's Promise, the organization created by General Colin Powell.

Now I travel all over the southern part of Oklahoma. I start Girl Scout troops in high-risk areas and areas that have never had Girl Scouts. I carry my medicine with me, but I don't take my breathing machine. If I get into trouble I have to go to the emergency room in any city. A small price to pay for what I've gained.

I'll never forget the day I went to one of my schools with a planned activity for the troop. We were going to paint our names in a unique way. One of the girls asked me if we had to do this. She never wanted to do anything I planned. She had a bad attitude toward me ever since my first visit. She had told me I was an "old maid" because I didn't have any children and I was already nineteen years old. My goal was to convince her that there was so much more to her life than having babies at a young age. I just didn't know how to reach her.

That day, I said to her, "If you don't want to paint your name, what do you want to do?" She said she wanted to help those kids who got shot in Colorado. She asked if we could make cards for them.

I ran out to my car and got the crayons. I was crying with joy knowing what a big step this girl had taken.

I want every girl—no matter where she is—to be introduced to Girl Scouts. I'm looking into starting a Girl Scout program in a homeless shelter and a prison. Girl Scouting is for all girls. The prison program will be for mothers and their daughters when they get together once a week for about an hour.

When I received my Gold Award (Eagle Scout equivalent), my family and friends gave me a life membership to Girl Scouts as a gift. They couldn't have given me anything more meaningful.

I look at my life and how it could have easily gone in a different direction—one focused on doctors, medicine, and precautions. Instead, I chose a life of scouting, of helping others, of a fun life filled with friends with emergency room visits in between.

I am convinced my breathing problems will never get the best of me. I'm convinced the hole in my heart is healed. It has to be—my heart overflows each time I make life a little better for one more girl.

To learn more about Girl Scouts, contact: Sooner Girl Scout Council, 224 South 14th Street, P. O. Box 1466, Chickasha, Oklahoma 73023. Tel: 405-224-5455 or 800-GSUSA-4U. Fax: 405-222-2502. Web site: **www.gsusa.org**

CHAPTER 14

Guardian Angel

MARIA PIÑEDO

ONE DAY MY MOM AND I WERE FIGHTING. She worked full-time as a waitress, so she always expected me to help take care of Kim, my six-year-old sister, and to clean the house—not much fun for a twelve-year-old. This particular day I was frustrated and I didn't want to do the dishes. I said, "Why do I have to do everything?"

She dragged me outside and put me in the car. She looked at me and said, "You know what AIDS is, right?"

I muttered, "Yeah, I know what that is. I heard about it on TV."

She said, "I have AIDS; Kim and I have AIDS. We have AIDS, Maria, and I can't fight with you anymore. I need you to help me." Then she went back into the house.

I remember sitting there stunned. I didn't know what to do. I didn't cry; I was just so scared.

Just the week before I had seen the AIDS quilt on the television. I saw names of people who had died from the disease. I thought, "This doesn't relate to me." And I had switched to cartoons.

Now, the two people I lived with and loved had AIDS. My mom had been infected before my sister was born, through a blood transfusion. This was back in the early '80s when they didn't check blood supplies.

My mom did not want me to tell anyone because she was afraid of people's reactions. After she told our church leaders, they asked her not to bring Kimmy back to Sunday School. She had gone to her church for support and instead found out they were afraid they would catch the disease.

So we kept it a secret and moved around a lot. I didn't have many friends, and that was really hard on me. My days were spent going to school, coming home to take my mom and Kimmy to doctor's appointments, paying bills, grocery shopping, cleaning the house, and taking care of them at night. I got frustrated sometimes not having a normal teenager's life. I wanted to do normal things, but this was my mom and sister. It felt right to be there with them.

After awhile I became less frustrated. For the longest time, every birthday I would wish for a cure, for them to be OK and not die. My wish changed as they got worse. I started praying to God, "Please, God, take them, and don't let them go through a lot of pain." It became more about loving the time I had with them and preparing myself for their deaths.

Mom and Kimmy went to the hospital more and more. I wanted to be with them, so I slept in a chair at the hospital; sometimes I was given a cot. Every time they went to the hospital I was sad and scared, wondering if they were going to die.

Eventually we contacted the AIDS Foundation. They were wonderful. They had counselors who came to the house. I could talk with them; they understood what I was going through. At fifteen years old, I finally had a support system and friends.

My last two years of high school I was homeschooled. It was too hard to go to school every day. The hospital stays were becoming more frequent and longer. The teachers knew about my situation and helped me with my assignments.

Kimmy passed away three years ago in the hospital. She was thirteen years old. I got a lot of support from the AIDS Foundation, but I did have to sign papers and make final arrangements. Mom didn't want to do it. She was too sick and it made her too sad.

After Kimmy was gone, my mom got worse really quickly. She had a brain infection and couldn't talk. Nurses taught me how to change her catheter and take care of her at home. They came to check on her every morning.

The day came when Mom didn't recognize me anymore. She mostly slept—she was on heavy pain medication. One night she was breathing really hard. I slept next to her all night, fearing the worst.

She died the next morning. Thank God the nurse happened to be there. I think I may have lost it otherwise.

I stayed at the house by myself for a month. I wanted to; I needed the time alone. I started packing things and had a garage sale. My friends from the AIDS Foundation were there for me helping any way they could.

These same friends are now my family. One very good friend—Kimmy's counselor—is like a big sister. She invited me to stay at her house. I've lived with her for two years.

I'm still sad. I miss Mom and Kimmy every day. But I'll be OK. I have a lot of friends and a lot of love. I'm in community college and love school.

I don't think AIDS will ever leave my life. It's part of who I am. I want to help educate as many people as I can. I participate in all of the Foundation events. I speak to students at colleges, high schools, middle schools, and elementary schools to educate them about AIDS prevention. Many schools are afraid to tell kids to wear condoms or practice abstinence. When I speak I tell them, "You really need to protect yourself. Don't be fooled. Just because someone doesn't look sick, he or she could still be infected. Don't assume your boyfriend or girlfriend is all right. And don't think it can't affect you." And then I tell my story.

I won't stop until there is a cure. I really hope we find one soon.

Share Maria's dream and join in the fight to end AIDS. Contact: Sacramento AIDS Foundation, 1330 21st Street, Suite 100, Sacramento, California 95814. Tel: 916-448-2437. Fax: 916-448-3568.

Also contact: The CDC National AIDS Hotline Tel: 800-342-AIDS; 800-344-SIDA (Spanish).

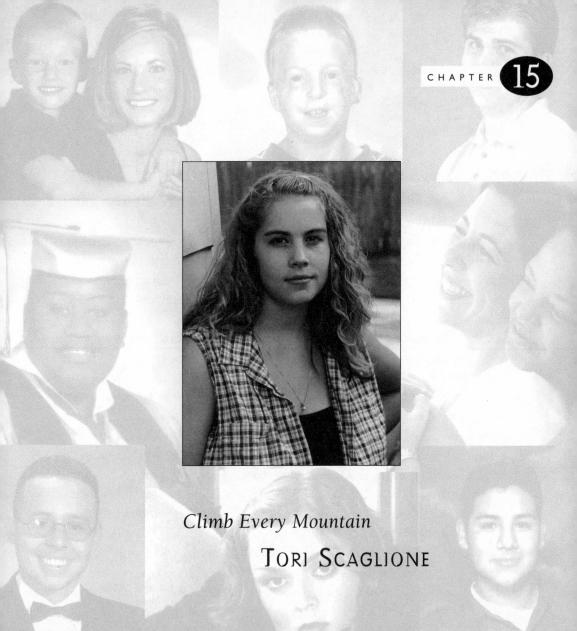

CHAPTER 15

Climb Every Mountain

TORI SCAGLIONE

On June 4, 1994, my boyfriend Sam and I were driving back to Des Moines after spending a couple of days trashed in a hotel. We had drugs and an unloaded gun in the car. I was sixteen years old.

We almost hit another car. The other driver started yelling at us, and Sam got angry. He turned the car around, grabbed the gun, and jumped out of the car. Bystanders were watching. I yelled at Sam telling him to get back into the car and to quit acting stupid. The other driver told me to "shut up." Suddenly he noticed Sam had a gun. He got into his car and drove off.

We had only driven about a mile and a half more when the police pulled us over. One of the bystanders said the driver had called them.

I was really drugged out—I was probably using about five ounces of coke a day along with acid. I was nasty looking; I weighed only 90 pounds and was covered with impetigo scars.

I took the unloaded gun in the car and hid it in my pants. The cops told me to get out of the car, then to get back in, and then out again. When I got out of the car the second time the gun fell out of my pants. They threw Sam to the ground and told me to get down. They found five grams of crack cocaine under the car when they went to tow it. They found a pipe in my pocket and around $300.

They handcuffed both of us and loaded us into separate cars. We were charged with possession with intent and carrying a deadly weapon.

They sent Sam to jail because he was legally an adult. From my understanding he was bailed out within forty-eight hours. They sent me to a detention center and then to a hospital for my impetigo.

I was then sent to a thirty-day drug treatment center and underwent an evaluation to see if I should be tried as an adult. If I got waived to adult court I'd be facing fifty-five years for possessing drugs and carrying a gun.

A month later I was free of drugs, away from Sam, and determined to stay clean. My lawyer and I arrived at the court hearing feeling hopeful. But they waived me to adult court.

I spent about three hours in Polk County Jail with convicted murderers until they sent me to a detention center. I was scared to death. I wasn't supposed to talk with Sam because he was a codefendant. But his mom would call the detention center and say she was my mom and then give Sam the phone.

The prison officials found out and knocked me down to the lowest level of offenders to receive privileges. I cried a lot, got mad, but I didn't really feel any emotions. I guess at the time I didn't care—I didn't care about much at that point.

I got into the Youthful Offender program—a program for nonviolent offenders for a first offense up to the age of twenty-two. I fell into that category because the gun wasn't loaded and I wasn't using it as a weapon. But to get into the program I had to sign a confession stating that I had drugs and a gun and they also belonged to Sam. They really wanted to nail Sam because this was not his first offense. Prior to this I had said the gun was mine, but that I didn't know anything about the drugs. After I signed the confession I got to move in with my mom.

I started to see Sam again, going against the no-contact order issued under the program. I was out running around, though I wasn't using drugs. But it was the same behavior—not doing what I was supposed to do to be on probation, acting erratically, and not very emotionally stable.

My probation officer and drug counselor decided that I violated my probation program, and I was arrested again.

This time I sat in the Polk County Jail for about three weeks with two murderers. During that time I was really down. My parole officer and drug counselor decided I could either go to inpatient treatment or stay in jail.

They let my dad take me up to Rockwell City, Iowa, where there was a drug treatment center. He took me over to my mom's house to pack my stuff to move. I climbed out the window and ran up the street. I hopped a bus and went to Sam's house without getting caught.

We left and went to his friend's house. Sam had an ankle bracelet that was connected to the probation office, so he couldn't miss curfew. When it was time to leave I climbed into the trunk of his car to go home—that way nobody could see me.

All of a sudden I heard Sam yell. My dad had found us. He grabbed Sam from behind. They fought and fought as my dad tried to get the keys. Finally my dad got the keys, opened the trunk, and found me. He took me back to his apartment and yelled at me. I was totally terrified.

Dad immediately took me to the treatment center. This was one of the worst places you could imagine. The first month they made me wear pajamas until they thought I was not a risk to hurt myself. They didn't let me wear shoes because they thought I would run away.

I hated the place. A group of us started sneaking around and breaking rules. I got kicked out because they said they couldn't do anything else for me. They said I was hopeless, that I would go to prison. They said my problem wasn't drugs. My problem was my personality.

My parents wouldn't take me back, so I was interviewed for acceptance at the Iowa Homeless Youth Centers (IHYC), one of the services offered by Youth and Shelter Services, Inc. I was accepted into one of the programs, the Buchanan Transitional Living Center, on February 27, 1995.

The counselors were wonderful. They knew everything about me, yet they were willing to accept me. The home was different than any other place I'd been. Other homeless girls and guys my age were very supportive. We were like one big family. Maybe the timing was right for me. My life started to improve.

During the time I was in Rockwell City, Sam was convicted and sent to prison. We were still in touch, but when my life got better I cut off all communication with him. I completed my GED. I got a job working at a fast food place downtown during lunch. And after work I went to my drug treatment program.

I met a guy in my treatment class. His name was John. We started seeing each other. We enjoyed going to movies, eating out, and visiting museums and exhibits—we were both through with the partying and crazy stuff.

He took me to his prom. It was the end of his senior year in high school. He was planning to go off to college in the fall, and I was going to stay in Des Moines and go to community college. Our relationship was just a fling since we were going our separate ways. I started having feelings for him but didn't want to tell him. I didn't want to get hurt.

The day before John graduated from high school, I called him, crying. He came right over. I sat down on his lap. He said, "Well, are you?" I started crying, hating to confirm what we both were afraid of—I was pregnant.

I told him that he could leave, that I didn't expect anything from him emotionally or financially. He looked at me and said, "It's my damn kid too."

John was really supportive. He went with me to my first doctor's appointment, and we spent a lot of time together before he left for school.

One weekend he came home from school. I showed him the videotaped ultrasound of our baby. He cried. He told me he was getting attached even though the baby was only five months in utero.

I finally told my mom and dad I was pregnant. My mom started talking about adoption, something I just could not do. I told my parents that I wasn't a little girl anymore. I went through a lot to finally get my life straight. They needed to respect that I needed to be my own person. They both understood and agreed to support any decision I made.

I dreaded telling my case manager I was pregnant. The transition living program did not let women who were over three months pregnant stay in the program. But luckily they were starting the Lighthouse Program, a program for pregnant and parenting women ages sixteen through twenty-five. So I still had a place to live.

In August John went to college and we talked once or twice a week, depending on what we could afford. I started school and got a job working at Sears. In November I moved into my own apartment through the program. John came home every other weekend to visit. I was going to Young Mom classes through IHYC. Both of us completed the Youthful Offender program and were on basic probation until the following year.

John was in town every other weekend. I went into labor and he was with me. We went to the hospital at midnight and our son, Asher, was born at noon on January 13, 1996.

John came home from college in February. He couldn't handle being away from Asher and me. He moved in with his dad until June and got a job working for his grandparents. I got a promotion at Sears to supervisor of a department.

The following semester we both went to community college. In the spring we were both off probation and done with all of the legal stuff. We got married in March! Three months later I was discharged from the Lighthouse Program. I applied for a staff position, hoping to give as much help to others as I received.

To think I'm a staff member helping other homeless pregnant girls is amazing to me—especially when most people thought I was going to end up in prison. I'm a youth specialist making sure the girls do what they are supposed to do—complete their GEDs, find daycare, get food stamps, to name a few of the responsibilities. I work overnight and facilitate a group called Voices, a self-realization group. I usually have an activity where the girls are working on themselves—how they can control anger or feel better about themselves.

I speak and tell my story for the United Way and for IHYC to help raise money to help other girls. I always tell young girls to try and prevent pregnancy at a young age.

I was in a theater group while I was pregnant, through Planned Parenthood, and one of the tee shirts we wore said, "Don't have a kid until you're through being a kid." I find that true. If you're not ready to be a parent, if you still want to run around and be stupid, don't have a kid, because you won't take care of your kid right.

I want others in trouble to know you are not alone, to see you can do something, that life's not so bleak. I want you to know you can succeed and rise above what everybody else thinks about you. There's a lot of help out there.

I look back on my life from the time I became an out-of-control teen. I started doing drugs simply because I was curious. Don't do it, even if you are curious. Curiosity killed the cat. I'm lucky to have made it—many people don't.

Youth and Shelter Services provides services for runaway and homeless youth, making it possible for them to soar to a brighter future. Contact: Youth and Shelter Services, Inc., P. O. Box 1628, Ames, Iowa 50010. Tel: 515-233-3141. Fax: 515-233-2440. Web site: **www.yss.ames.ia.us**.

- If you've run away or need shelter call:
  Covenant House at 1-800-999-9999.

- For information on a Planned Parenthood Clinic near you, call:
  Planned Parenthood at 1-800-230-PLAN.

Sears Photo Studio 1999

Watch Out; Help Out

HORACE POLITE-COBB

Hᴵˢ ɴᴀᴍᴇ ᴡᴀˢ Dᴡᴀʏɴᴇ Cᴇᴅʀɪᴄ Mᴀʀᴛɪɴ. He was on the football team and he was our fastest runner, so they nicknamed him Cheetah. He was in my sixth-period gym class. That particular day, he wasn't there, and I didn't think anything of it.

When the bell rang, everyone went out to catch the buses. I was out there on the ramp as usual, talking with my friends, and the next thing I knew, I saw Cheetah running as fast as I've ever seen him run before. He was running directly in front of me. I saw this other guy running after him. He had a small, blue duffel bag in his hand, and there was something black in the other hand. It didn't register with me what the black thing was. At the time I didn't think anything of it.

I walked down the walkway after them, and Cheetah tried to turn the corner, but it had been raining the day before and the ground was a little slippery. So he slipped, allowing enough time for the other guy to catch up with him. The guy shot him right there, in front of everybody—200 or 250 high school kids, the principal, teachers, the resource officer—just *bam,* right there.

When Cheetah fell to the ground, the guy jumped on him and pistol-whipped him in the face. Then he got up and dropped the gun, and one of our coaches jumped him and held him down. They called for more people to help; the resource officer came over and handcuffed him.

They really couldn't clear out the area where Cheetah got shot because everybody was just crying and running around. It took probably five hours for me to register what had happened. Then I thought, "Man, that could have been me. I mean, the gun could have accidentally gone off and hit me. They passed right in front of me. I could feel the wind from them."

The day after, they called counselors from other schools. For two or three days these counselors made themselves available to help everyone emotionally.

For the next week, everything was just quiet. Usually the lunchroom was loud, kids acting obnoxious, but now it was like a ghost town. We had a memorial service in front of the school. Everyone brought candles, and we prayed and sang songs.

They found out later that the guy who shot Cheetah, Antonio, had a female cousin who he'd been talking to, saying that he was going to do it. The girl had gone to our school resource officer and told him that she thought her cousin had a gun. But I guess the resource officer didn't pay it too much attention since that type of stuff doesn't happen in Savannah very often, especially at my school. So I guess he really didn't take it to heart.

After Cheetah's death, my friend, Monica, went to an all-day community-service fair a local community center was sponsoring. Nonprofits from across the country came to distribute information and to get people to join. A man by the name of Vernon Jones, who worked for Youth Crime Watch of America, was there, and he introduced the program to her. It's a program where students police themselves. She told me about it and I thought, "Something needs to be done, and obviously a school resource officer isn't the answer, because if it was, then this wouldn't have happened. Who better to know what's going on in the school than the students themselves?"

We met with Corporal Warren Pippen of the Savannah Police Department. Officer Pippen let us use his office to have Crime Watch meetings and discuss the things that we wanted to do. Then we held a kick-off program at school, and it went well. Johnny Lawson, from Auburndale, Florida, did a skit called, "A Walk

Down Death Row." Two guys are on the basketball court "going at it," and one guy is beating the other one, 21–0. The one who loses gets so mad, he goes and gets a gun and comes back and shoots the other guy. I played the part of the guy who did the shooting, and I had to put on this prison attire—this loud orange jumper—and I was even handcuffed.

I never had handcuffs on in my life. It was very uncomfortable and made me think of a lot of different things—like suffering the consequences of things I do in my life. I never really thought about that before.

I began to rethink my goals. Before the shooting I focused mainly on academics—honors courses and good grades. Life was so much more than that. I felt the need to do whatever I could to help eliminate youth violence.

Since that day, I took the Youth Crime Watch Program under my wing. It's become a part of my life. I'm involved with it on a national level—speaking and advocating nonviolence all over the country—and probably will be for a long time.

Once youth and youth advisors are trained in Youth Crime Watch methods, they take ownership of their program for their school. Some of the key components include mentoring and mediation, conflict resolution training and application, drug and crime-prevention education, and anonymous crime reporting systems. So when a situation comes up, and a student sees a friend or anybody getting into an altercation, they can help them out without making it seem like they're police. They'll say, "I know you are angry, but think about the consequences before you react. I'm just like you. Let me show you a better way to handle this situation."

Our program works. That's why we were able to get the program in almost every public school in Savannah—that's seven high schools, eight middle schools, four elementary schools—about twenty schools. And there are also two private schools involved.

Here's an example of how we work things out. Say there is a boyfriend and girlfriend. The girl catches the guy with another girl and they all go to the same school or hang out together. Say the girls get into a fight. A teacher will send them to the office and maybe recommend them getting suspended. But instead of them being suspended, we recommend that the Youth Crime Watch Program be implemented. We would say to the principal, "Wait a minute, before you suspend them, give them an opportunity to talk to us first, and maybe we can solve this before any further action needs to be taken." If it's two girls who are fighting, we'll get two other girls to do the mediation. The first thing is to introduce the mediators and lay down the rules. We tell them, "You talk to me, not the other person, because that cuts down on arguments. Only one person at a time talks. If we don't resolve it here, then we'll let administration handle it, and you know what will happen if administration comes in."

We make sure to have them sign a paper agreeing that no one is going to lie—that everything is going to be the truth and everything said will be confidential. Then we give each a chance to tell their story. After their story, we try to get them to talk about their feelings, "How did you feel when she did that, or when he did that?"

Once they get their feelings out on the table—many times it's just a misunderstanding—the mediations are real short. It's important to get the feelings out, and once that's done and they get a chance to kind of vent, it pretty much works out. If it comes to a point where they still don't want to be nice to each other, we make them agree that they won't even look at each other, won't speak to each other, won't even breathe on each other. That's better than fighting and getting suspended. That's usually an absolutely last resort, but if it comes to it, then that's what we ask them to agree to.

After that, we usually have a follow-up, maybe a week or two later, to see how everything is going. After the follow-up, we usually don't have a problem with the kids again.

My goal is to get the Youth Crime Watch Program in every single state in the United States. Right now, we're in eighteen states, and some U.S. territories, like the Cayman Islands and Guam.

Unfortunately, there's still going to be youth violence even if we have a Youth Crime Watch in every school in America. But we can decrease it to a level so low that many lives could be saved. I know there's at least one person in every single state that has the ability to get this going. That's all it takes—one person.

For those unfortunate souls who have witnessed youth violence, we need to give them some inspiration to keep on, because the memory is going to be with them forever. It can affect a lot of things they will do in the future, and it could hurt them a great deal. I think about the shooting at my high school. The thing that kept my head up was the program. It gave me something positive to look forward to when I arrived at school every day.

Imagine if Antonio and Cheetah went through the mediation process. That one probably would have been a little difficult, but I think we could have handled it because I knew Cheetah. I think he wouldn't have teased or bothered the guy if he'd known how much this was bothering him. Antonio had had a rough childhood. He'd been in and out of the juvenile system since he was thirteen or fourteen. He was fifteen at the time he shot Cheetah. It was nothing for him to shoot Cheetah, because he'd already given up on life.

There's always a life out there that needs our help. That's why we have to stay with it, no matter what.

Join students like Horace who practice peaceful conflict resolution and live by their "Watch Out; Help Out" philosophy because they care. Contact: Youth Crime Watch of America, 9300 South Dadeland Boulevard, Suite 100, Miami, Florida, 33156. Tel: 305.670.2409. Fax: 305.670.3805. Web site: **www.ycwa.org**.

CHAPTER 17

Lifetouch 1999

That's What Friends Are For

BRANDEE TERRELL

THURSDAY, AUGUST 7, 1997, WAS THE FIRST DAY OF SCHOOL at our high school. Usually it's the best day—you get a new schedule, you find out which friends are in your classes, and you meet your teachers. But this particular day proved to be the worst ever.

After school, my friend Jeremiah went with his brother, Harley, to a birthday party for their friend Krystal. Harley left the party early to baby-sit his nephews and nieces. Krystal's mother drove Jeremiah home when the party was over.

It was 9:30 P.M. when they stopped in front of the driveway to turn left. Someone was coming from the other direction. The guy in the truck was going at least 70 miles per hour. His truck slammed into the car. The force of impact turned the car and truck 180 degrees, shoving the car into a ditch.

Jeremiah's parents, Linda and Dan, heard the loud crash and ran out to help. They had no idea their son was in the car. When they got close to the car they heard Krystal say, "Linda, it's Jeremiah."

Jeremiah's dad couldn't get him out of the car, so he climbed into the wrecked car and held him until the ambulance got there. Jeremiah was pronounced dead at 11:02 that night. He suffered massive head injuries. He was only fourteen years old.

The driver who killed Jeremiah never hit his brakes. There were no skid marks. Texas law on the books at the time stated that intoxication is an alcohol level of .10. His level was .204.

The man was arrested for intoxicated manslaughter. His bond was set at $10,000. He was able to get out of jail with $1,000. He left the area, never to be seen again.

Jeremiah wasn't in my grade—he was a couple of years younger—but when you live in a small town like Valley Mills, Texas, you know everyone around you. And news travels quickly.

I couldn't believe my friend was dead. He was the kind of guy who made everyone feel good. He liked you for who you were. He didn't categorize you—whoever you were, you were his friend. I couldn't believe I saw him at school earlier that day, laughing, and in an instant a drunk driver killed him.

I couldn't stop crying. So many thoughts and feelings came over me: If only they'd left the lake a few minutes later; how much I would miss Jeremiah; how I hoped the driver would be punished for life; how unfair life could be; why would this happen to someone as good as Jeremiah.

His death was devastating. Yet it brought the whole town together. The church where his funeral was held 700 to 800 people, and it was full. It was a celebration service. It was a time to celebrate the life he lived, the life he loved so much.

Afterward we all went to the graveside. Jeremiah was a strong believer. He would not have wanted us to be sad. During the service, people read poems and were given the opportunity to share.

One of the kids who came to our school only a year before remembered his first day. Jeremiah was the one who came over to them and said, "Hi, how's it going?" He made him feel comfortable, made him feel he was important in a new place.

Another friend talked about how much Jeremiah loved to play the trumpet. He played in the marching band at school. If you lived in Valley Mills all you had to do was walk out your front door and you'd hear him practicing almost every day. He played "The Star Spangled Banner" every year at our Fourth of July celebrations in the park.

At the end of the service the music director played "Taps" and the Boy Scouts released multicolored balloons. I watched the balloons float up toward Jeremiah and somehow knew he was OK.

My mom took me over to his house to pay our respects. I couldn't even imagine the shock and pain Jeremiah's parents were going through. When I got there, I reached out to hug Linda, and she hugged me back—we held on to each other for at least ten minutes. I just wanted to take a little of her sadness away. But it was Linda who helped me through my anger and tears.

We began spending a lot of time together. She got involved with MADD— Mothers Against Drunk Driving. She and Dan were dealing with their son's death and the news that the truck driver was nowhere to be found. He never showed up for his court dates. She wanted to come to school to speak to all of the students— to discuss Jeremiah and drinking and driving. She asked me if I would consider also speaking—she felt the kids should hear a peer's thoughts.

I was really nervous. I'm very active in school, and usually I don't think twice about getting up in front of people. But I knew this speech would be different.

I'll never forget that day. I stood up in front of all of the students, took a deep breath and began, "Think about getting into a car and driving after you've been drinking. Could you live with yourself if you killed a family member or a friend? Don't think it won't happen to you. Look at Jeremiah. He was so good, so innocent."

Then I went a step further. I told them I chose not to drink at all. After so much pain, I didn't see the point. My friends and I hang out, but we go to movies, go camping—we find other things to do.

The reaction to my speech could have gone either way—kids could have made fun of me or really could have taken it in. Afterward, I walked down the hall to class. Kids looked at me and smiled. Even if it was only for one day, I know they heard me. A couple of my girlfriends said, "We're not going to drink anymore."

Maybe that promise only lasted a short while, but at least they don't drink and drive.

After speaking I felt better about Jeremiah's death. The deep sadness within me lifted just a little. Standing up for Jeremiah eased my pain.

Linda and I continue to speak at events and schools all over town and in surrounding towns. Our MADD chapter gives us information to share. As the literature says, "Alcohol is not a magic potion. It doesn't make you look good, appear cool, or feel courageous. It simply robs you of your mind. You can't leap buildings in a single bound. You probably can't even hurdle the sofa. Alcohol isn't really all it's cracked up to be."

I feel older than my seventeen years. Losing Jeremiah made me see life differently. There are no guarantees. I realize the importance of letting someone know how much you value his or her friendship. You never know what may happen. Nobody is promised they'll make it through anything bad that happens. But anybody can promise to care enough about people and life not to cause anything bad to happen. Don't drink and drive.

Help stop drunk driving today. If you need assistance locating the chapter of MADD in your community or want information about MADD, call: 800-GET-MAD. Web site: **www.madd.org**.

In Canada, contact: MADD Canada, 72 St.. Leonards Avenue, Toronto M4N 1K3. Tel: 416-644-9666. Fax: 416-480-2038.

Help unite youth to combat underage drinking, drug abuse, and impaired driving. Provide a community awareness program and promote the use of the student–parent contract and party guide. Middle schoolers, promote the program called Students Against Doing Drugs. Be the athlete in your school who introduces Student Athletes Detest Drugs. Students Against Driving Drunk (SADD) Executive Director: William Cullinan, P. O. Box 800, Marlboro, Massachusetts 01752. Tel: 508-481-3568. Fax: 508-481-5759. Web site: **www.geocities.com**.

CHAPTER 18

For the Love of Learning

ARUNDEL BELL

B Y THE TIME I REACHED FOURTH GRADE, I KNEW I was not at the same reading level as my friends. Reading even a simple book was a struggle. Assignments in class took me a long time to finish. My teacher, Ms. Agnew, talked with my parents and suggested I get tested at Texas Scottish Rite Hospital in Dallas, Texas.

The testing was an all-day process. Two days later the doctor said, "Arundel has a learning disability. She has comprehensive dyslexia."

Then the doctor said, "Some of the smartest people are dyslexic. Did you know Albert Einstein and Winston Churchill were dyslexic?" This information made me feel good, because both men were so successful in life. They must have learned how to compensate for their dyslexia.

My mom and dad jumped into action. I went through elementary school and middle school working with tutors and taking remedial English classes. My parents read to me or we read together many nights.

I decided early on that I was not going to sit around pretending I understood something and not learn anything. I tried books on tape, but I found having a reader worked better for me. I could see their lips, see their expressions, and read along silently with them.

I never hesitated to ask for help. I remember going to camp every summer and getting letters from family and friends. I asked my friend, Leslie, to read me the letters. Every day when the mail came she sat down on my bed and read to me, never laughing at me or making a comment about me to anyone else. I think it's because I could say to her, "I really need your help. Read to me."

Reading was a struggle because I couldn't sound out words. For the longest time I couldn't spell *necessary*. I finally had to ask somebody what the word meant. I saw it so many times. I memorized the word because my friend made up a little song to help me spell it. She helped me learn how to memorize it. I can't remember the song, but she always sings it to me whenever I see her.

One time when I was with my brother, Barron, and we were driving by a Jack-in-the-Box restaurant. I asked him, "What are julapinos?" He told me the word was *jalepeños*. We had a good laugh over that one and many other mispronunciations, but never in a way that made me feel inferior.

Barron never thought his accomplishments made him better than me. My brother received a Presidential Scholarship at A&M; he also won a National Merit Scholarship. I was so proud of him. My parents never compared us. They never said, "Your brother's better because he makes better grades." They did not judge us on performance. Yet they always encouraged us to do our best.

When it came time for me to apply to colleges, I wasn't choosing where to go—I was just hoping to get in *somewhere*. After lots of tutoring, I took the SAT with extended time. I scored high enough to get into a special program for students with learning differences that many colleges offer.

I began my college career at Texas A&M University. I use adaptive technology—my textbooks are read aloud to me through a computer. The program also highlights important information and arranges the information so I can understand it. I get the information through three senses: visual, auditory, and kinesthetic. I need all three ways to process the information.

The program is called the Texas Text Exchange. It was first conceived in 1995 by David Sweeney, who is currently Coordinator of Adaptive Technology Services (ATS) at Texas A&M University. ATS realized that text-to-speech technology could be used as a good alternative to books-on-tape. Texas A&M was the first to offer a comprehensive e-text scanning program for students with learning, attention, visual, and neurological disabilities.

The Texas Text Exchange maintains an online digital library of e-texts. Any student with documented learning differences can access the program for free—any student in college anywhere in the world! All the student has to do is go to his or her special needs department at the college and ask for the program. The disability service provider at the school can contact the Texas Text Exchange and become a member.

Recently I transferred to Southern Methodist University and am still using ATS through their special services. I know that ATS makes it possible for me to succeed in college. I still work with tutors daily. I'm at a low reading level, but I keep going.

I take my education very seriously. My parents, brother, teachers, tutors, and friends make a great support team. I want to do well not only for myself, but for them, too. If they are willing to help me, I'm willing to show them I can do it.

I was one of the lucky ones. I was tested and diagnosed properly. Texas Scottish Rite is such a wonderful place for physical and mentally challenged kids. Any child can go there for free.

I decided to volunteer at Scottish Rite so I could help others as much as I was helped. One day I read a book to a little girl in a wheelchair. I read the book very slowly so she could understand the story and the words. A nurse came in and said, "It is time for you to leave. It is time for her medicine."

The girl then said to me, "Thank you for reading the book to me."

I walked out of the room with a huge smile. Here I was, able to read and make someone else happy at the very place that changed my life.

I also go to elementary schools and talk with students. At one, the principal explained to me that students with learning disabilities feel badly about themselves and often drop out of school. So I tell the kids, "It's all right to have a learning disability. You can make it. You just have to be able to find out the best methods for you to learn. Find things in life that will motivate you. Life is a learning experience. Always ask for help; never be embarrassed if you don't know something. Feel bad if you don't ask."

I also tell kids, "I took my driving test four times, but you know what? Every time I didn't pass I cried, went back home, and got that silly book out and made myself study it until I passed. It's OK to cry and feel frustrated. Crying makes you feel better. But, if you fail and you don't do anything about it, then you've really failed. You can always succeed if you just keep trying."

It doesn't matter where you are located. If reading is difficult for you and you want to use adaptive technology, ask the Special Services department of your school to contact: Texas Text Exchange, c/o David Sweeney, Adaptive Technology Services, Hart Hall, Ramp B, MS 1257, Texas A&M University, College Station, Texas 77843-1257. Tel: 409-845-0390. Fax: 409-862-1026. Web site: **http://tte.tamu.edu/.**

In Canada: Learning Disabilities Association of Canada, 323 Chapel Street, Suite 200, Ottawa, Ontario KIN 7Z2 Canada. Tel: 613-238-5721. Fax: 613-235-5391. E-mail: ldactaac@fox.nstn.ca. Web site: **http://educ.queensu.ca/~lda.**

CHAPTER 19

Jostens 1999

The Ripple Effect

TALLI OSBORNE

] WAS BORN A QUADRUPLE AMPUTEE.] HAVE NO ARMS AND ONLY HALF OF EACH LEG. My calves and feet are attached to my hips, but I don't have thighs or knees. I have nine sisters and ten brothers. My parents adopted all of us. Some of us have disabilities, and we come from many different ethnic backgrounds. Yet we all have one thing in common—we were chosen to be part of an awesome family.

My sisters and brothers came from foster homes, group homes, and adoption agencies. When my parents adopted me, I was living in a hospital in Montreal where I was born. I was a healthy baby, but I stayed at the hospital because my birth mother didn't keep me. The hospital had a great foster program. I'm told I had my own room, and nurses and staff loved taking care of me—I was too young to remember.

To accommodate twenty children, my parents bought a big home on a few acres of land. It has eleven bedrooms, and I've shared a room with my seventeen-year-old sister Miriam since she was adopted.

Miriam has arthrogryposis. She has full hands and arms, but she can't move them. And her legs don't bend all of the way because her knees aren't fully formed. She wears splints on her legs. The doctors thought she would never walk, but she can because she wanted to. Her legs hurt sometimes during the day, but she doesn't care. She refuses to use a wheelchair.

I have mio-electric arms, but I don't wear them anymore. I wore them up until eighth grade, but when I started high school I wanted to be more independent. The arms were really heavy and got in my way. I can do more without them on. I do wear prosthetic legs. They're like extensions, like stilts. I put my feet into the prosthetics, and then I have an artificial leg and foot. I can run around fine without them, but when I wear them they make me taller.

I have never let my disability get me down. Sometimes I get frustrated over little things, but it's not like I go into a deep depression. I've seen other people with even fewer disabilities than me, and they let the disabilities consume their lives. I want to tell them, "You know what? Live with it."

There's a saying, "Treat her as if she's like everyone else." Why wouldn't people treat me like everyone else? I am like everyone else. Arms and legs don't define who I am. My attitudes and behaviors reflect who I am.

My mom and dad have always told me it doesn't matter if I am physically challenged. If I want to do something badly enough, I can do it. They have never made my disability an issue.

When I was younger and wanted to write, I used my feet. It never occurred to me to think, "Oh my gosh, I don't have hands. How am I going to write?" I just picked up a pencil with my feet like someone with hands naturally picks up a pencil. When I got older and began to wear prosthetic legs, my own feet were covered and I couldn't use them to write. I tried different methods until I found one I liked. I wrote with the pencil in my mouth for a while, but I didn't like the taste and it restricted me from being social. I tried putting the pencil between my shoulder and chin, and that worked. That's how I write now, and it's really easy. In class I take notes just like everyone else. Teachers have offered me extensions on assignments, but I've never taken one.

I've never let someone else feed me. When I was younger I used my mouth instead of fingers to pick up food and didn't think twice about it. As I got older I tried different ways that looked more acceptable. I put the fork in my sleeve and that worked great until I started wearing tank tops. Now I pull my bra strap down and it holds my fork perfectly. You can find ways to do anything as long as you think creatively.

For many years I did need help getting dressed. It's hard to pull up your pants if you don't have arms. I'm a social butterfly, and when all of my friends started having slumber parties I wanted to go. But I wasn't going to let my friends dress and undress me. To fix this I worked with a lady and designed a stick with hooks on the end. No one has dressed me since. I can even stick a razor on the end and shave my legs.

My friends know that I like to do things for myself. They don't ask me if I want help because they know I'll ask if necessary.

I have lots of friends. We hang out, go to punk concerts, and have fun partying. My disability is not a big deal—nobody cares. I think it's because of my positive attitude. I always make jokes about myself. One day I was at rehearsal for our upcoming school musical production, and one of the guys held up a glove. He said, "I found this glove. Anyone missing a glove?" I yelled, "Yeah, it's mine." We all started laughing.

I find that if you joke around, with anything, everyone around you becomes more comfortable. I know if I was always sad, complaining, and angry, feeling like I was cheated out of a "normal" life, others would feel sorry for me. I wouldn't like that at all. Chances are, I wouldn't have many friends either. Who wants to be around an angry, bitter person, with or without arms and legs?

I've learned how powerful having a positive attitude is. It's important to me to share my experiences and practical tips with young children who are amputees. I want kids to know the only real disability they face is a poor attitude about themselves and life. It's easy, if you don't mind working a little harder than most, to physically adapt. The challenge is the ability to adapt emotionally.

I am very involved with an organization called the War Amps of Canada. When amputee ex-servicemen returned from serving in World War I, they formed a group to provide counseling, self-help skills, and practical tips. Seventy-five years old, War Amps is still a strong organization providing programs and services to Canadian amputees and their families.

I love working with the young kids who are in the CHAMP program—Child Amputee Program. The kids in the program are kids either born with limbs missing or kids who have lost limbs in accidents. The program provides financial assistance for artificial limbs, supportive counseling programs, and regional seminars.

The seminars bring child amputees and their families together from all over the country to meet each other and see that there are others facing the same challenges. We network and gain financial and emotional support. We learn about different artificial limbs, and children demonstrate their own special limbs for different activities, such as swimming or playing a musical instrument. It's also a time for the children to have fun and play with other children who are missing limbs.

The War Amps CEO, H. Clifford Chadderton, lost his leg below the knee in 1944 while he was in charge of the Royal Winnipeg Rifles, battling in Belgium and Holland. He has devoted his life to War Amps, giving hope to as many child amputees and their families as possible.

Mr. Chadderton is a living example of hope. When he was sixty-six years old he learned to downhill ski. He decided to make a film inspiring amputees to take up the sport. An entire series of award-winning ski films grew from one of the first productions, *The Nakiska Kids*.

As a junior counselor, I try to be a role model for the kids. I share practical tips I've learned and encourage them to live their lives to the fullest. I tell them to try everything. Things they think would be impossible can be accomplished. If they really want to do something, they can do it.

For children with multiple amputations, like myself, there's another program, called Super Champs, that's provided by the War Amps. Education is stressed, and kids are started on computers at a very young age. The War Amps believes that computer-literate amputees will be given better job opportunities as they compete for jobs in the workplace against non-amputees. The program, JUMPSTART, provides financial assistance for children to buy computers. That's how I was able to get my laptop.

I remember helping a little girl learn to use a keyboard with her artificial fingers. When she started typing by herself, her entire face lit up. She didn't stop smiling. I'm not sure who was happier that day—she or I.

I just graduated from high school. I'll be going away for university, but I plan to continue helping child amputees.

The examples set by my parents are proof of how beautiful life can be and the ripples it creates when you choose to live life to the fullest and give life to others. My nineteen brothers and sisters and I thank you, Mom and Dad, for the gift of life.

Discover all of the exciting programs available for child amputees in Canada. Contact: The War Amps, Key Tag and Address Label Service, 1 Maybrook Drive, Scarborough, Ontario M1V 5K9. Tel: 800-267-4023.

National Limb Loss Information Center is an information clearinghouse that provides comprehensive resources for people with limb loss, as well as their families, friends, and the health care professionals involved with their lives. Contact: Amputee Coalition of America, National Limb Loss Information Center, 900 East Hill Avenue, Suite 285, Knoxville, Tennessee 37915-2568. Tel: 888-267-5669. Fax: 423-525-7917. Web site: **www.amputee-coalition.org/**.

Sumner Photography 1999

Young or Old, Big or Small,
AIDS Affects Us All

ALLISON WIGNALL

I BECAME AN AIDS ACTIVIST AT THE AGE OF TWELVE AFTER LEARNING that my adult friend, Toby Richard, was struggling with AIDS. I met Toby when we acted together in the stage play *Annie* at the Ingersoll Dinner Theater.

At the audition the director told everyone he had already cast Toby as FDR, and he was living with the AIDS virus. The director wanted to let the parents and the prospective actors know.

I'm sure some were apprehensive when they heard about Toby, but I wasn't scared because I didn't have any idea what AIDS was. To me Toby was simply a tall, thin guy who didn't have any hair.

Over the course of the summer we became friends. Toby was extremely positive and funny and took full responsibility for his illness and the quality of his life. "Allison, your life is really important. Live each day to the fullest, make the most of each day and treat people well," he'd say.

After the play's run was over, he asked me to sing with him at the All-Iowa AIDS Benefit. He had the most gorgeous tenor voice; I couldn't believe he asked me to sing with him!

We dressed alike and sang "It's a Grand Night for Singing." We caught the audience off-guard—I was the youngest kid to ever perform there. Our song must have touched their hearts because tons of people started putting money in the collection tubs, and we finished to a standing ovation.

After that I kept in touch with him. I wrote him letters and sent him gifts—an *Annie* pillow, and a heart bookmark that said, "I'm always with you, you're always loved, this keeps me close to your heart."

As the years went on, he became very sick, so he didn't call or write as often. In one of the last letters he wrote to me, he said he was planning his funeral. Toby explained it was going to be a special event, a celebration of his life, and he hoped I would be able to attend.

A few weeks later the phone rang very early in the morning. It was right before school—no one ever calls that early—and somehow, I knew what the call was about. Still, when my mom told me Toby died, I couldn't believe it. No matter how much I had prepared myself for his death, it was still painfully hard.

His funeral was exactly what he planned—a perfect finale to his life. His mom made a beautiful quilt of Toby and his dog, and it was displayed at the front of the church. Music Toby enjoyed was playing, and during the service anyone who wanted to get up and tell stories about him did—some quite sad, others very funny. One person told us that as Toby was dying, family was all around him. At one point Toby had said, "Would you please leave me alone? I'm trying to die here." We all laughed—this was so Toby's style.

After the service we had cake and punch. Everyone was handed a white balloon. We went outside where the sun was shining, and the clouds swirled angelically. We were told to put our thoughts, feelings, and love in our own balloon. We released them at the same time—all these white balloons floated up to heaven to Toby, as if to say good-bye for one last time. I knew from that moment on, Toby would be with me always.

I vowed to continue his fight to educate others, to raise money, awareness and hope for those who struggle with AIDS and HIV. This wasn't easy.

Watching Toby go through his illness and physically horrendous changes scared me. I knew I didn't want to get AIDS, nor did I want to have to live through more death, and I was certain if I got involved in helping other people who had AIDS, sooner or later I'd lose them, too.

I knew in my heart it would be wrong to let my fears keep me from helping others learn about the risks and causes of AIDS. So when I was asked to be the keynote speaker and singer for the All-Iowa AIDS Benefit the year after Toby's death, I took a deep breath, thought about Toby, and said yes.

Since then I've continued my fight against AIDS. I sing at the benefit each year, speak to service groups, walk in AIDS walks, participate in statewide and national AIDS awareness events, and served as Honorary Chairman of the AIDS Project Fundraising Campaign. I made a presentation to the Ryan White Foundation for the Kid's Hall of Fame induction ceremonies at the National Geographic headquarters in Washington, DC. I spoke and sang in honor of Ryan White, who was the first child to bring a face and a name to AIDS. I put on a benefit concert for Whitney Williams, another child who touched many lives with her courageous battle against AIDS. I recorded an album which contains a song entitled, "Don't Let AIDS Take You Away," written by my dad in memory of Toby, which I've sung at the NAMES AIDS Quilt Memorial Dedication, at benefits, and on television.

I speak to students and tell them, "If you know someone with AIDS, be a friend—be tolerant and compassionate. You can't get AIDS by being a friend. Make good decisions, live by good values, and educate yourself about the disease. Your education is very important; school is very important. They're all stepping stones to bigger and better things in your life. Helping other people—doing little things, like opening a door for your mom when she's carrying groceries, smiling at someone in the hall at school whom you don't even know but who looks like they're having a bad day, or saying something nice to somebody—makes a big difference in people's lives. It will make your life better, too. Kindness has a ripple effect."

In the past six years, along with the AIDS Project and the All-Iowa AIDS Benefit, I've helped to raise about $350,000 for Iowans living with AIDS and HIV.

Until there is a cure, there is still much to be done. By working together, we can make a difference. Young or old, big or small, AIDS affects us all.

Toby's parents came to my high school graduation party, which was really a great surprise. After Toby died, they gave me back the *Annie* pillow and bookmark I had sent him. The gifts were worn; I could tell he used them.

Now, when I look at the pillow or the card I think about the wonderful, funny, talented, positive man—who showed me how to live life to the fullest—and I realize how miraculous life can be.

Join Allison in her fight against AIDS. Contact: AIDS Project of Central Iowa, 508 10th Street, Suite 200, Des Moines, Iowa 5030. Tel: 515-284-0245. Fax: 515-282-7787. Or contact: All-Iowa AIDS Benefit, P.O. Box 305, Des Moines, Iowa 50302. Tel: 515-288-2622. E-mail: IABENEFIT@aol.com

For statistics and general information about HIV/AIDS, contact: National AIDS Hotline. Tel: 800-342-AIDS.

CHAPTER 21

Believe In Who You Are

MARIO GONZALEZ

MY MOM, SARA, AND DAD, GUADALUPE, WERE BORN IN ZACATECAS, MEXICO. Along with my sister, Mirna, and my two brothers, Alex and Adrian, I was born in the United States. We are the first generation of our family born in the United States. Our parents cannot read or speak English.

We live in the lower west side of Long Beach, California. Our family has lived here for twenty years. This is a low-income, dangerous neighborhood. It has a pretty bad reputation from gang warfare. I used to crawl into my mother's room every time I heard gunshots. I never knew if a bullet was going to come through our window.

Like any child, I wanted to go outside to play, but I knew it was too dangerous. Ever since I was a small child I wanted to move away from the neighborhood. But we couldn't afford to move.

My stepbrother, who's ten years older than me, lived with us. He was a former gang member and spent time in and out of jail. I didn't see him very much, but when he was home he treated me very badly. He called me names and said hurtful things to me.

As I got older, things got worse. I was ashamed of my parents because of their background. I cried all of the time, wishing that my parents could speak my language. I was in middle school and I wanted to be like the other kids with parents who spoke English, participated in school activities, and did things together as a family.

I started to claim I was half-Italian and half-Mexican. My sister found out and lectured me about my pride. She told me I should be proud of all of the struggles our parents went through for us.

At the time, though, all I wanted was to feel like I belonged. I knew I didn't want to join a gang. After experiencing the pain my stepbrother brought to my parents and me I vowed to myself, no matter how lonely I felt, that I would find acceptance in a positive way.

Then my cousin, Dorina, happened to invite me to a meeting of an organization she was in at school called M.E.Ch.A—Movimiento Estudiantil Chicanos de Aztlan. The president of the club, Diana Bernal, announced three upcoming events she wanted everyone to attend. She said that they would motivate us and make us proud of our struggles as a race. We would be going to UCLA, USC, and California State University at Long Beach to visit the universities and meet with Chicanos attending those schools. She reminded us of the philosophy of the club, that political involvement and education were the best avenues for change in Chicano society.

I couldn't believe what I was hearing. I had wanted to find a positive direction in my life. I had wanted to feel like I belonged somewhere, and suddenly here was a group for me. This was like a dream coming true!

When we went to the universities, the Chicano students told us we should be the best we can be. We attended workshops motivating us, as first-generation kids, to go to college.

I started going to all of the M.E.Ch.A. meetings. Latino or Chicano speakers came to discuss their occupations. A lady named Diana Perez, a city employee from the Department of Health and Human Services of Long Beach, told us about a program she had just started. This program, called S.T.A.R.S. (Students Talking About Resisting Substances), needed volunteers to become peer educators to help teach middle school youth about drugs and alcohol. I immediately volunteered. I was trained and after a year I wasn't a volunteer anymore because I was hired part-time!

The following year, as a tenth grader, I became president of M.E.Ch.A. Diana Bernal introduced me to a teacher at school named Ms. Hernandez. Ms. Hernandez wanted me to know about a youth program called Youth Leadership Long Beach (YLLB). This program was a program for the youth in the city of Long Beach to help develop leadership skills. I applied. Only thirty students were chosen, and I was one of them.

Youth Leadership met for nine months. Only seventeen students graduated from the program because you couldn't be absent more than two times. I wasn't absent even once; I received a certificate for perfect attendance.

Before I could graduate I had to complete a project. Our group chose to conduct a teen forum, to help make the youth of Long Beach aware of organizations that they could get involved in. I was excited about the project because I knew how life-changing good information could be.

We passed out flyers, called people, and got donations for the food for the guests and the youth at the forum. Lots of students came. Watching them sign up to join different organizations made me wonder if perhaps any of them were feeling like I used to. Maybe I had given him or her the gift my cousin had given me— an awareness of a new direction in his or her life. If so, I would consider the forum to be a huge success.

Eleventh grade was the best year of my life. I got my driver's license, bought my own car, and met my first girlfriend. I worked for the Long Beach Department of Health and Human Services facilitating an HIV/AIDS prevention program called TLC—Teens Living Carefully. It was a four-session class teaching youth about HIV transmission, setting limits in a sexual relationship, condom negotiations, and decision-making skills.

This year, my senior year, I am associated student body president of my school. I had to campaign for the position and I won. I oversee the freshman, sophomore, junior, and senior classes and their class officers.

When I look back at the scared, confused middle school boy who was embarrassed to admit he was Chicano, I barely recognize him. When I'm working with teens who are looking for direction in their lives, I always say to them, "Get involved. Join a club or join an organization that interests you. Don't let anything or anyone stop you from believing in yourself. The only way for you to believe in others and make our world a better place is for you to first believe in you. Today really can be the first day of the rest of your life."

Find out how to start a M.E.Ch.A. chapter and help promote higher education, culture, and history. Contact: M.E.Ch.A. Tel: 310-206-6452. Web site: **www.angelfire.com/nt/lacmc/HF.html.**

CHAPTER 22

Olan Mills 1999

Go for the Gold

MICHAEL MUNDS

]'VE HAD ABOUT SEVEN SURGERIES ALREADY, AND] AM ONLY TWELVE YEARS OLD. I was born without a chin, and I really didn't have much cheekbones, so they redid those. My ears were just skin, and right now the doctors are working on them. They're using ribs. Ribs grow back until you're eighteen years old.

My mom told me what I had—Treacher Collins Syndrome—when I was little. She never tried to keep it a secret. She has the same birth defect as I do. She had to go to a special school for the hard of hearing, and she didn't want that to happen to me. I have a special hearing aid—a headband—called a "bone conduction hearing aid" that allows me to hear. I get to go to public school.

Mom and I went to different kinds of schools, but we both know about being teased. I don't get teased much. But, if I do, I stand up for myself. I'll say, "It doesn't matter. You can make fun of me. Tomorrow it could be you." They usually stop laughing, and some even say they're sorry or they didn't mean it. I tell them to just not do it again. If someone has a problem with me, it's his or her problem, not mine.

I may not always fit in, but I try to stand up for what's right. I'm always trying to help someone else. I even postponed a surgery in 1995 because of the Oklahoma City bombing. I saw the bombing on TV and decided to do something.

I wanted to raise $20,000 to help the victims. My mom wanted to knock it down to $10,000, so I agreed. My mom asked my grandpa to help, and together they wanted to knock it down to $5,000. This time I said no—my goal was $10,000.

I planned a bowl-a-thon. To announce it, I made banners and started going out asking for sponsors. I got bored going house to house. I didn't raise very much money that way. So I told my mom I wanted to try car dealerships.

My mom and I walked into dealerships, and every time we went in, a salesperson said to my mom, "May I help you?"

She said, "No, talk to him."

I told the salesperson my plan and asked for his or her help. I don't think anyone said no. The car dealerships provided a lot of money.

Lots of people came to the bowl-a-thon, and we had a big banner for everyone to sign. The governor of Colorado, Governor Romer, also signed it. Then I flew to Oklahoma and handed the governor of Oklahoma, Governor Keating, a check for $37,000 and the signed banner. We made $27,000 over our goal!

I also started the 168 Pennies Campaign for Oklahoma in Denver. The number stands for the number of bombing victims in the Oklahoma City bombing. This project is a nationwide effort in which school children donate pennies to help pay for the building of the children's section of the Oklahoma City National Memorial—a national memorial for the victims and survivors of the bombing. The memorial will have 168 empty glass and stone chairs, one for each person who died.

I was able to get the word out about the campaign through my grandfather. He's my best friend and a reporter for the *Inglewood Herald*. Also, the superintendent for the Denver Public Schools put out a call for donations on the Internet. There was a competition among the schools. Money is still coming in. Right now I have around 500 pounds of pennies, quarters, dimes, and nickels in my living room.

I've already taken $1,100 to Oklahoma for the memorial. On that trip I met a lady whom I adopted as my aunt. I call her Aunt Fran. She was in the building across the street from the Federal Building during the bombing. The force blew the glass out of the windows. She was sitting in her chair and got covered with glass. She used to wear contact lenses, but the force blew the contacts back into her eyes, and she has eye damage now. She's already gone through a lot of surgeries. She wants to have laser surgery to get rid of the scars. But you don't see them unless you look really closely.

Another new friend from Oklahoma is a man named Randy, to whom I write. He was in the Federal Building, and his hand was on the door ready to go out. They say had he opened the door he would not be here today. When I heard about Randy, I had to write to him.

If I hear about or see someone hurting, I have to help. Like the bowl-a-thon for Baby Allie. After I saw her on local TV, I wanted to help raise money for research to find a cure for her disease—spinal muscular atrophy. I bowled fourteen games by myself—the most I've ever bowled. I had blisters all over my hands, but I raised $2,500 for Baby Allie.

She died just short of her first birthday. That was tough. I missed going to visit her, holding her little hand, and seeing her big smile. I sent her mom a card. On it I drew a vase of flowers with an angel. You open it up and there's a beautiful star. I wrote, "She's never far away. All you have to do is look up and she's there."

I've done fund-raisers for the AIDS walk-a-thon, Arapahoe Advocates for Children, Loving Hands "Unlimited," and the Sewall Child Development Center. When I heard about Kosovo, I raised money and donated it to the Red Cross in honor of the Columbine students.

I have raised over $87,000 to date, and my goal is to raise $100,000 by the time I am thirteen years old. Why do I spend my time raising money? I believe everyone can make a difference, and it doesn't matter how old you are, or who you are, or if you feel you are different, because everyone is different in one way or another. Some differences are on the outside and other people can see them, but some differences are on the inside.

People wonder if I'll become a professional fund-raiser or a professional bowler. I really don't know. But I do know one thing: Don't put yourself down. If people are laughing at you, reverse it. Laugh at them or with them. You can stand up for yourself. You can't let anybody push you around. You won't get anywhere. If you're sad or mad, don't be. Be a little upset, but don't waste the day. Find someone to help—you'll feel a whole lot better when you bring a rainbow into somebody's life.

Share Michael's belief that one person can make a difference, the younger the better. In memory of Allie and in the hope of finding a cure for spinal muscular atrophy, contact: Eyes of Hope Foundation, 1129 East 17th Avenue, Denver, Colorado 80218.

Join Michael and help build the children's section of the Oklahoma Memorial. Contact: 168 Pennies Campaign, Oklahoma City National Memorial Foundation, One Leadership Square, Suite 150, P. O. Box 323, Oklahoma City, Oklahoma 73101. Tel: 405-235-3313.

If you want tips on how to be a successful fund-raiser, contact: Michael Munds, 3411 East Colorado Avenue, Denver, Colorado 80210.

CHAPTER 23

On Wings of Love

YESENIA NIEVES

ONE NIGHT MY STEPFATHER GOT REALLY ANGRY. My three brothers and I always slept together in one room. That night we were all laughing and playing. He came in and told us to be quiet. We kept on playing, and he came back. This time he hit us with a belt. He hit my finger with the buckle and dislocated it.

The next day at school my teacher asked me what was wrong because I couldn't move the finger. It hurt and it was swollen. I told her the story, and she called the Department of Corrections for Youth Services in Bridgeport, Connecticut.

They called my mother to make an appointment, because they wanted to talk to her and they told her to bring me with her.

We both went, and after meeting with them, we began therapy for a while. The therapist would tell us to just let our feelings out. We started to communicate a little better, but we were never that close. I told her if something happened at school, but I never told her how I felt about my stepfather.

Why would I? She always took his side. When she saw or heard the beatings and him screaming at me, she'd tell him to leave me alone. But she never mentioned a word about it to me later, when he wasn't around.

I think she was afraid of losing him and his paycheck. She felt the best way to keep peace was to go along with whatever he said.

I do remember one time my mom went the distance for me. My stepfather was in Puerto Rico, and she let me go to a party with my friends. I was thirteen years old at the time. I was never allowed to go to another party until my prom.

Growing up in that house was like being in prison. I thought about taking pills or choking myself—just to end the pain. One time I did take pills, but I didn't take enough to do anything. Neither of my parents ever knew I took them.

I did always think about running away. But I didn't have the courage to do it.

My mother's need for me to take care of my two little brothers was what changed my life. I left school early each day, took the bus to my brothers' school, and met them when school got out. We would walk across the street to the South End Community Center and waited for my mother to get off work and come get us. Other kids my age might resent having to do this every day. I was just glad I didn't have to go home.

Even though the programs at the center were free, my mother would not sign us up. So my brothers and I sat quietly in a corner, and I helped them with their homework. They sadly watched the other kids having fun, wishing they could join in.

One afternoon, the executive director, Jo Anne Rodriguez, came over to us. She said, "Why are you just sitting there? Why don't you sign up and become involved in the programs?"

I told her we weren't allowed. Jo Anne then spoke to my mother, explained the programs, and convinced her to let us participate. She even got my mother to pick up my brothers at the usual hour and let me stay two hours longer until the teen program ended. Jo Anne drove me home every single night.

After six months I trusted Jo Anne; every time she said she'd do something for me, she did. She always followed through, so one day I told her how awful my stepfather was and how my mother let it happen. I told her I just couldn't take it anymore.

We cried. She hugged me and said, "You can always count on me to be there for you."

She kept her promise. She helped me get a job and get money for college.

When I turned seventeen, Jo Anne encouraged me to apply for SNAP (Safe Neighborhood AmeriCorps Partnership), a community service program designed to reduce crime, violence, fear, and drug-related problems in Bridgeport. If I were accepted, I would receive a stipend for providing services to agencies with youth programs. One of the agencies happened to be South End Community Center. The program also offered an educational award to attend college.

Jo Anne explained SNAP to my mother. The hours were longer at the center. She promised my mother she would still bring me home—I just wouldn't be home until 9:30. My mother agreed to let me apply.

I'm proud to say I'm now a SNAP worker helping high-risk kids at South End Community Center—the same place that gave me my life back.

Through their Positive Youth Development program, I help address the needs of high-risk children living in the neighborhood. One project I am responsible for is called STAR (Serious Teens Acting Responsibly). The first part of the program is about helping kids with their own special concerns. We answer their personal questions as best we can.

The second part of the program empowers kids ages thirteen through seventeen to help others. They become Junior Aides to the younger groups. This is called Youth Helping Youth: they tutor, conduct workshops on teen pregnancy and gang violence, teach baking and karate, and help on field trips. They become the teachers.

I don't think I would have made it without Jo Anne's help. My senior year I finally got to go to a rock concert. She was the one who told my mother, "Yes, Yesenia is going to the concert. I gave her the ticket as a graduation present. I'm taking her, staying there with her, and bringing her home." Jo Anne also convinced her to let me go to my prom. Jo Anne paid for the ticket and drove me both ways. My date was not allowed to pick me up, but at least we got to be together at the dance and I got to wear a beautiful dress—one I bought with my own money.

I graduated from high school and told my mother I was moving out. A SNAP staff member offered her attic apartment to me. I was "of age," and my mother couldn't stop me.

I hope no teen has to grow up in a home like mine. If you find yourself in a situation like mine, find someone to talk to. Don't hold your feelings in. Get help. Jo Anne's love and advice worked. I am living on my own, going to college, working at South End, and having fun. I am finally free.

Get involved in a community center in your neighborhood. For great programming ideas, contact: Jo Anne Rodriguez, South End Community Center, Inc., 650 Park Avenue, Bridgeport, Connecticut 06604. Tel: 203-331-0200. Fax: 203-331-0809.

Find out how you can serve and make a difference. Contact AmeriCorps. Tel: 800-942-2677. E-mail: acorps@infosystec.com. Web site: **www.americorps.org**.

CHAPTER 24

Hal Wagner Studio

The Only Vote That Counts

NIKKI BINZ

SACRED HEARTS SCHOOLS, WHICH ARE ALL-GIRL CATHOLIC PRIVATE SCHOOLS, are nationwide. In ninth grade I started going to one of their schools, Villa Duchesne, in St. Louis. I didn't make new friends right away. The girls weren't very involved in school clubs, and there appeared to be a lot of apathy. I knew making friends was going to be a challenge.

I had heard how much fun the girls had on weekends. When a few of the girls started inviting me, I was so excited. I was finally being included.

What I didn't realize was that every time I had heard, "The party was awesome. We had so much fun," the party was really a group of kids hanging out to drink. The big attraction was alcohol.

I went to a few parties and tried to enjoy myself even though I didn't drink. I tried to have friends who did drink or who did drugs, but it wasn't working. We would talk, but it was awkward. I felt they didn't want to be associated with me, and I didn't really want to be associated with them.

Pretty soon I started making excuses as to why I couldn't go to a party. I would tell the girls that I already had plans. After a while they figured out I wasn't going because I wouldn't drink, and they quit inviting me.

It was frustrating—I didn't understand what the big deal was. Why was alcohol a part of every social event? Why weren't the parents doing anything about it? Why were parents opening their homes to kids, providing kegs, and letting the kids drink?

I just never understood the hook to alcohol. It seemed really dumb to me. First of all, it's illegal. I'm someone who follows rules; I guess you'd consider me a "good girl." Also, I value my health. I love sports. I play golf and run track, so why would I want to start drinking and risk ruining my health and my ability to play sports?

I made a couple of friends, but I felt isolated in a world where most of the kids didn't exist—in a drug-free and alcohol-free world.

That's why I couldn't believe my good fortune when I was chosen to attend a leadership training conference. I was introduced to an organization called TREND—Turning Resources and Energy in New Directions. TREND is one of the programs the National Council on Alcoholism and Drug Abuse (NCADA) offers in St. Louis. Here I was, hearing about a new organization with opportunities for leadership, community involvement, and drug-free fun for students in grade six through college. I was meeting other kids who wanted to have fun in a drug-free atmosphere. For the first time in a long time, I felt like I belonged.

As crazy as it sounds, given that I was in the minority, I decided to start the club at my school. I convinced the couple of friends I had made to start it with me. Even though most of the kids drank, I felt that if I offered an alternative social scene, some of the girls might stop drinking and join the club. And the small percentage of girls who didn't drink would have a group to hang with.

We tried a variety of activities—bowling, hockey, and basketball games, and haunted houses. We promoted our events, but only about ten girls showed up for each event. Five of those were the original club members.

After an event we'd ask if they had fun, and the girls always said yes. But, we couldn't get them to join. They didn't want to be associated with TREND. They felt it was a "dorky" club and they couldn't really agree with the hard stand against alcohol.

My parents knew what a difficult time I was going through. They suggested that perhaps the sacrifices I was making for TREND were too great. They thought that maybe I should give up my leadership role in the club.

I told my parents I would not quit. I wanted kids to hear from other kids, not adults, the importance of drug-free, alcohol-free living. The TREND National Coordinator, Ginny Shaller, suggested that our club focus on younger classmates if our peers were not interested in a prevention program. This was a great suggestion. Our membership increased to twenty-five.

To get even more members, we decided to create a citywide TREND chapter with kids from all of the area high schools. We named our new group SMASH—Student Movement Against Stupid Habits.

Our first big event was a party. We called it Party in a Big Field and held it at a local park. It was awesome! Bands played great music. We had a bonfire and hayrides and we ate hot dogs and drank sodas. About 300 kids came.

The party was from 7 P.M. until 11 P.M. Usually, when there's a party without alcohol—such as a school-sponsored dance—kids come, but only for a short time. They leave to go to a place where they can drink. But almost everyone stayed the entire time.

About twenty-five girls from my school came. They may have come because they were friends with the guys in the bands, but at least they came. I even heard that some of the girls were saying, "TREND isn't too bad."

Unfortunately, none of them joined SMASH or TREND. So I still didn't have many friends my own age within my school to hang with. And since the kids in SMASH were from different schools and we all lived pretty far from each other, we only got together for our events.

Our next big event was during the Christmas season. About thirty of us went Christmas caroling and collecting money to buy gifts for kids who were in the Cardinal Glennon Children's Hospital during the holiday season. We bought gifts and delivered them to the kids.

I learned an important lesson that day. I saw a very sick child lying in a hospital bed with all sorts of tubes going in and out of her. When I walked into her room, she greeted me with a big smile. She welcomed me and laughed and talked to me as if she'd known me forever. She wasn't thinking about what was wrong with her. She was making sure I felt comfortable being there.

I left there realizing I was spending way too much time frustrated that most kids didn't want to be a part of a drug-free, alcohol-free group. I needed to redirect my focus. I felt a lot better *helping* others rather than trying to *change* others.

With my new understanding, I looked for more community service opportunities. Our school sent me as a representative to a national Sacred Hearts conference in New York City—where girls from Sacred Hearts schools all over the nation got together to help the homeless. There I participated in one of the best weeks of my life. There were about sixty girls. For a week we worked in soup kitchens and homeless shelters. I got to know a homeless woman named Sue who came to the soup kitchen every day. She told me how hard her life had become—how she had lost her home and her job and how badly she felt having to come to a soup kitchen for free food. She was trying to get her life back together.

I have never felt more grateful in my life. Having parents and a loving home became quite precious to me. I came back home determined to do whatever I could to help others. We at TREND collected items for five adopted Bosnian families. We even were able to get a family a stove!

I became president of both my school TREND chapter and the citywide chapter. Representing both, I went to my first National TREND Conference. It's a three-day training conference every summer. Once again, I met lots of great kids devoting their time to making their schools and communities a better place.

I interned at the NCADA-TREND National Conference on Prevention, where I organized activities, entertainment, and even led two complete workshops.

The TREND chapter at my school still has very few members. It's a big commitment in high school to join a drug-free, alcohol-free club—it's not the most popular choice a teen could make.

My friend, Ginny Shaller, wrote this poem and sent it to me:

Trendsetters Have the Right Stuff

A HEART that pulses with passion for life and compassion for others.
A BRAIN that can tell the difference between what is good and bad,
and what is fair and unfair.
A MIND that thinks for itself regardless of peer pressure.
A BACKBONE that supports your convictions and values.
MUSCLES that give you inner strength and support a healthy body.
EYES that visualize possibilities, stay focused on your goals,
and see the good in every person.
EARS that listen to your conscience, are open to the ideas of others,
and are closed to gossip.
A NOSE that can smell the beautiful things in life.
A MOUTH that vocalizes your beliefs and speaks with optimism and kindness.
LIPS that deliver kisses and smiles.
SHOULDERS that hold your head up high when you stand up
for your convictions and accomplish your goals.
A STOMACH that cannot tolerate injustice and
explodes often with belly laughs.
HANDS that offer help and applaud the achievements of others.
FINGERS that point to you when it is your duty to assume responsibility.
FEET that will take you to your dreams.

It's a challenge to take an unpopular path when you're a teen. A choice I made that I thought would ruin my high school years turned out to be a choice that gave me the best high school years I could ever have had. I am now a freshman at the University of North Carolina. I like who I am and how I live my life. And really, that's the only vote that counts.

Establish a student-led, drug-free TREND chapter in your school. Contact: Ginny Shaller, National Coordinator, TREND, 8790 Manchester Road, St. Louis, Missouri 63144. Tel: 314-962-5124 or 800-666-5124. E-mail: trend@ncada-stl.org. Web site: **www.ncada-stl.org/trend/infosht.htm**.

CHAPTER 25

Full Circle

CAROLINE SHRAMM

AS SOON AS WE ARRIVED, I REGRETTED MY DECISION to come to Remuda Ranch, a treatment center for anorexia in Phoenix. I cried my eyes out. I begged my parents, "Please take me back home with you. I promise I'll eat anything. I swear I will." They were crying, too, but they walked out the door without me.

I was a junior in high school going through a living hell. The nurses went through my stuff before I could unpack, and that really bothered me. I couldn't talk to my parents for the first three days. They tube-fed me at night because I was down to eighty-five pounds. I pleaded with them to give me food instead, but they wouldn't because they said my body wouldn't be able to handle it.

After a month they began to give me more food. I started to adjust because I made friends with most of the girls. It felt good knowing I was not alone in this—we related so well to each other. In group therapy, we discussed how we used food so we could show people we had something of our own that nobody could take away. Eating was one part of my life my parents could not interfere with—no one could force me to eat. The sad joke of it all was that my survival technique was killing me.

I told the girls in the group how my anorexia started. When I was sixteen I started eating healthier foods and not as many snacks. I started to lose weight and liked how I looked. I would look at a girl on TV or a model in a magazine and love how thin she looked. I would tell myself, "I want a perfect body like hers. I want to look as beautiful as her," never knowing I was looking at airbrushed pictures a majority of the time.

My junior year of high school I really went downhill. I barely had breakfast, didn't have lunch, and didn't eat whenever I didn't have to. I didn't throw up or use laxatives. I just starved myself and exercised. The more weight I lost, the more powerful I felt.

My friends knew I had a problem, but I tried to hide it. I was lying to everyone. I would tell my parents I was going out for dinner. My friends and I would get to a restaurant, and I'd tell my friends I ate at home.

I continued to get thinner and thinner. People began to call my mom to make sure I was OK and eating.

My mom would try to get me to talk to her. I just couldn't talk to her about it. This was my secret. My dad would try to help me by begging me to eat—sometimes even forcing me to eat. They just wanted to help, but I only got worse.

I began to wonder if I was crazy. It was like there were two sides of me. One of them was saying, "No, no, you can't eat." The other side would say, "Yes, you can—eat this."

I went to see a psychiatrist. I talked to her, but that didn't really seem to be going anywhere. I asked her about places to go—treatment centers—for eating disorders. That's how I ended up at Remuda.

During group sessions, I learned the importance of expressing myself, not holding anything in. I also realized I needed to find something else to make me feel special and in control—something that was good for me.

I returned home knowing how much the group sessions helped me. So I decided to create a support group for people with eating disorders. I called ANAD—the National Association of Anorexia Nervosa and Associated Disorders. They sent me information packets with brochures and newsletters and lots of information on eating disorders. I wanted to stay connected with others who were going through the same thing.

I called the Baylor College of Medicine and asked if they had support groups for eating disorders. They didn't. I told them my story and said, "I really love groups because I get to talk to other people who have the same problems. It helps me get everything off my chest that I need to. I really want to start my own group."

They loved the idea and found five girls who were interested.

The six of us meet once a week and talk. We talk about how it's going; we talk about life. We talk about small stuff too. We have somebody else to talk to and we feel better about ourselves.

By listening to another girl's problems and offering solutions, I know I'm helping myself. One of the girls decided to stop eating again. I heard myself tell her she needed to realize why she wanted to do this—to find out what the real problem was. I heard myself tell her to tell her mother or someone she can trust about it—not to hold it in.

I heard myself and smiled. Life is pretty amazing.

ANAD operates an international network of support groups for sufferers and families, and offers referrals to health care professionals who treat eating disorders across the United States and in fifteen other countries. For information on a support group in your area or guidance to start a support group contact: ANAD, Box 7, Highland Park, Ilinois 60035. Tel: 847-831-3438. Web site: **www.anad.org**.

Remuda Ranch is a caring place for women and adolescent girls who are suffering from anorexia, bulimia, and related issues. The Ranch is a restful oasis in which to reflect, replenish, rediscover, and recuperate. There is hope and help. Tel: 800-445-1900. All calls are confidential.

CHAPTER 26

Thorton Studios

A Living Legacy

JOHN SERRANO

T WASN'T UNUSUAL FOR MY DAD TO TRAVEL BACK AND FORTH from our home in New York City to Puerto Rico. He loved the island and made enough money to visit often. But this time he was gone for three months.

At first we thought he was just staying over there and not calling—he often would be gone for long periods of time. We would tell him it hurt us a lot, but he'd leave anyway.

Finally my mom called the police. They checked hospitals in Puerto Rico, New York City, Brooklyn, and Manhattan. My mom told them he had a tattoo on his arm. They checked for "John Does" with his description.

One day soon after my mom called the police, she met me after school. She looked really nervous and said, "Johnny, what would you do if something really bad happened to Poppy?"

I said, "What do you mean?"

She told me he was in a very bad car accident and in serious condition at the hospital. I couldn't believe it.

I went to see him. I hesitantly opened the door to his room. He was on life support and had all kinds of tubes in him. He was bald, with stitches all the way from the left side to the right side of his head. They had had to do reconstruction on his head.

This was not my father. To me, my father was an outgoing fisherman—he was Superman. He used to work as a bartender in a high-class restaurant in the World Trade Center. He got paid well. He also worked in construction for a while.

I couldn't believe this had happened. I sat my mother down. I told her I was only thirteen and I needed her to tell me how this happened. I felt like she was hiding something from me—she acted like there was more to the story than just a car accident. I asked her how she expected me to deal with this if she didn't tell me everything.

She explained to me that my dad used drugs at times, and this was the reason he got into an accident. He was crossing a big highway in New York while intoxicated. A car struck him and kept going. Then another car hit him. The police said they don't know how, but he got up and started walking. Then a U-Haul hit him and sent him soaring into a light pole. That just about demolished his entire cranium.

At first I blamed my mom, and then I started blaming myself. I felt that if I had known about the bad stuff he was doing, I could have stopped him from doing it. I just thought I had the power to do that. Maybe I could have made a difference.

My dad got better at first, but then he went into a coma. He was on life support for about seven months. I visited him often. The doctors told us to talk to him to try and wake him up.

He did eventually wake up. But he had brain damage and lay frozen in a fetal position. He was breathing on his own, but he couldn't recognize people and he couldn't speak. He was tube-fed. They moved him from the hospital to a nursing home.

In the beginning I used to go see him every day. Someone would pick me up after school, and I'd go and talk to him. I had to be there for him. We were two peas in a pod. Before, he was always on the move. He was never a person to sit down, much less be in a wheelchair. I knew he was suffering.

For a while I used my art to get out my stress. I expressed myself on paper— I would just draw to relieve my stress. Before my father was injured I went to him with everything. There are certain things a guy just can't go to his mom with. But,

I didn't have my father anymore. I didn't have anyone to talk with.

The pressure got to me. Seeing him like this really stressed me out. I wasn't able to do anything. I stopped going to see him every day. I went once a week, and then I started going very infrequently. I got tired of hearing, "He's got a fever, he's doing better, he's not doing well. . . ." I couldn't take it.

This went on for three and a half years. In his last few months I only visited twice a month. He finally died from a fever—a really high fever.

I fell in with negative people. I even tried drugs once, but I didn't like it. I thought at the time, "Oh my God, what am I doing? I don't want to end up like my father." It bothered me to think I took my pain to that level.

I started writing graffiti for a while. That's what the friends I was hanging out with were doing. I felt secure with them—I had an identity—so I thought it was cool to do whatever they did. I used to talk to them about my problems, about my father.

Many nights we stayed out on the streets all night long. Once when I got home at 5 A.M., my mom was waiting for me. She was crying and screaming because I was out late, and she knew I was out writing graffiti.

She told me this was not how she raised me. She didn't know why I was doing this. Why wouldn't I just talk to her?

I told her to leave me alone. I told her I didn't want to talk to her. I took out a lot of the aggression I had over my father's accident out on her.

My mom eventually remarried, and my stepfather treated me well. He tried to help me. He said, "You know John, you're going to grow out of this, hopefully. But what are you doing?"

I just cursed him out. I told him to get out of my face. I yelled at him that I didn't want to speak to him, and my life was none of his business. I told him he was not my real father and he needed to leave me alone.

All three of us started to cry. No one said a word. My mom came over to me with her head held down. She grabbed me and hugged me. Then my stepfather hugged me.

Crying, I said, "I'm not that bad."

They told me they were there for me.

I went to my friend's house. I said my mom was really worried about the things I was doing. He just said, "Don't worry, she'll get used to it."

Right then something clicked in my head. I thought, "How could this woman who brought me into the world ever get used to me putting her through all of this stress?" What was I doing?

I realized my mother and stepfather could have kicked me out. I owed them my life for their patience and understanding. I stopped hanging out with my friends the very next day.

I was already in a hole at school. My entire freshman year was totally out the window. I did all right, but not to my potential. I started doing better. I started getting involved with after-school programs. I did backdrop sets for the dancing, singing, and drama clubs in my school. I designed all of the stage sets for the drama studio.

One late afternoon I met up with an old acquaintance of mine, Jeffrey Rodriguez. He went to a different high school, so we rarely saw each other. We both had stopped to get haircuts on the way home. While I was waiting to get my haircut, I was looking at my art. He noticed my work and said he didn't know I drew. I told him I'd drawn since I was three years old, that my father taught me, and I told him what happened to my father. We had a long conversation.

He said he airbrushed. He said it was really fun and I should try it. He gave me his number and told me to come around and see some of the stuff he did.

I couldn't believe his work—it was beautiful. He used a compressor and a small air gun to paint and draw. The paint goes into a little bottle that you attach to the spray gun. I thought, "I've got to get into this." The very next day I bought my own airbrush. I started to practice, practice, practice.

In the beginning I airbrushed a lot of scenery because I liked the effect the airbrush gave you—lots of gradients or blends of colors—for horizons and sunsets.

As I airbrushed I thought about my father. He introduced me to the beauty of the sky. When we went fishing we'd see lots of horizons. We went fishing before the crack of dawn because it's the best time to catch fish. We would go out on the boat in the middle of the night and wait for the sun to come up. As soon as the sun came up, we would cast our reels.

While we were on the boat he taught me how to draw. He used Silly Putty. He stretched it out a little bit, put it on a newspaper, and made a big image. He made me trace the image. He taught me how to hold the pencils, how to follow the lines to get curves. He would teach me about all the different kinds of fish, and then I would draw them.

By the time I was five years old, I was drawing by myself and loving the feeling. I wasn't great, but I could feel the texture of the paint or ink or charcoals. Just to feel it inside was magical. It's almost as if I would become the paint, ink, or charcoal.

My airbrushing got better the more I practiced. One day Jeffrey came by to see my work. We talked about how too many kids in our neighborhood were out in the streets selling drugs. We thought wouldn't it be great if we taught art to these kids? It would get them off the streets, and maybe we could sell some of their work and make some "good" money for them.

That's exactly what we're now doing. We received a $1,000 grant for the project. We have to do three things: (1) We have to run the business by ourselves; we can't be helped by any adults. Adults can help as advisors but not with the

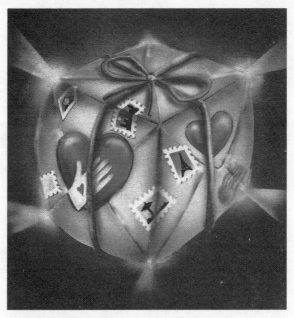

Artwork by John Serrano

handling of the money. (2) The project has to help the community. And (3), all the money received has to go straight into the business—we can't put anything in our pockets.

We have a studio where kids come to class. We meet once a week on Wednesdays from 4 P.M. until 6 P.M.

The kids love it. They're off the streets, doing something positive, and feel good about themselves. We try to show them that if they have a skill and are motivated, nothing can stop them. With skill and motivation, you can take your life to a whole new level—wherever you come from.

I made a solemn oath to myself to do something in my father's memory with my artistic talent. Helping a kid stay off the streets and giving him a positive experience is exactly what my father did for me. His legacy lives on.

In loving memory of my father, John Anthony Serrano, Jr.

Want to start an art program for children in your community? Contact: Latin Artists, 105 Chambers Street, 2nd Floor, New York, New York 10007. Tel: 212-571-4189. Fax: 212-571-6874.

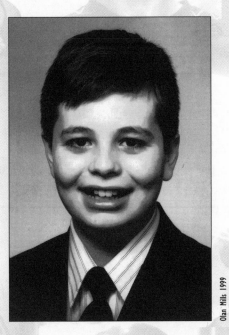

Olan Mills 1999

The Cello Cries On

JASON CROWE

M Y GRANDMOTHER, NANNY, WAS MY BEST FRIEND. She lived with us; she always laughed and played with me, read to me, and listened to me talk about all my ideas and interests, from video games to World War II. She always told me, "Don't say something about somebody unless that something you're going to say is something you can tell them to their face."

She always accepted me just the way I was. When I went to school—I'm home-schooled now—I got made fun of a lot. Like when I was in first grade, I was into rocks. I would dig in the pea gravel at recess and find fossils. The kids wouldn't believe me when I said I had found a crinoid or other fossil.

I was kind of like Rudolph the Red Nosed Reindeer. He had a red nose. My red nose was that I was interested in things different than my peers. In first grade I was reading books on Greek mythology—not the typical first grader's books of choice.

Nanny understood me. I knew, no matter how my day went at school, I had a friend who loved me. When she contracted cancer and died, I lost it. I was nine and a half years old.

I would cry at the drop of a hat—any little thing would anger me, and I couldn't concentrate on anything because my mind kept going back to Nanny. I became a nervous wreck. As much as I tried, I couldn't move her death out of my mind.

My parents were beside themselves trying to figure out how to help me get better. They went to an educational conference and heard a psychologist say that helping someone else when you feel helpless actually helps you feel better. They shared this with me when they came home.

At the time I was feeling helpless, like I had no control over my life. Something *had* happened I couldn't control: I couldn't stop Nanny's death. I thought about my parents' advice for a while. Nanny was an avid reader, so I figured the best way to pay tribute to her was to start a newspaper.

I started it on my old 386 computer. It began as a neighborhood newspaper. It had video game tips, stuff like that. One segment was called "Star on the Rise." I put a photo of a neighborhood kid in the paper and wrote a two- to three-paragraph story about the kid and what his or her current activities were, to build the kid's self-esteem.

I sold the newspaper for $3—that was for a three-month subscription. I went around my neighborhood to sell it and gave all the profits to the American Cancer Society.

Soon neighbors and relatives told their friends and relatives, and more and more people subscribed. The newspaper is now sold in twenty-eight states and fifteen foreign countries and is used by classroom teachers!

I'm only twelve years old. I don't think I would be publishing my own newspaper without Nanny's influence. Everything she and I talked about is reflected in the paper. I write about racial unity, peace and harmony, science, and geography. I include book reviews, and also I have a special column called "Kid Power." I feature kids who are making a difference in today's world. I have this segment to convince other kids they can make a difference. Because, in my opinion, anybody can—especially a kid.

One of my friends sent me a story about a Bosnian cellist. On May 27, 1992, a man was looking out his window at a huge line of men, women, and children gathered in front of a bakery. The bakery had just received a supply of flour. In this city under siege, bread was a rare commodity.

As the man was watching, a mortar shell fell right into the middle of the line. Twenty-two innocent people were killed.

Now this man ran outside and started to help the wounded, carrying them to ambulances—just helping the victims. When the ambulances went away, he was left with the feeling that he had to do something, but what could he do? He wasn't a doctor, he wasn't a soldier, he was Vedran Smailovic, principal cellist in the Sarajevo Opera Orchestra.

The next day, at the exact time of the bombing, Mr. Smailovic went outside and opened fire. His weapon was his cello; his ammunition was his music. He played beautiful music every day for twenty-two days—one day for each of the people who died.

I knew I had to do something to keep this story alive. I wrote about Mr. Smailovic and about religious intolerance and multicultural harmony. I organized a cello concert at the University of Evansville with twenty-one cellists and an empty chair representing Mr. Smailovic.

I also organized a memorial service on the fifth anniversary of the massacre. It was a congregation of people of different races and religions to share their creative energy.

But I had a bigger plan. I decided that I would commission a statue. I would send it to Bosnia as a gift from the kids of the world, like France sent us the Statue of Liberty. The statue would be a life-sized representation of Mr. Smailovic playing his cello.

The statue is a way for kids across the world to work together for a common cause—lasting world peace. It empowers us to bring awareness to the world.

I'm working hard to get the statue built. Authors, educators, musicians, and entertainers from all over the world are supporting the statue—Joan Baez, Yo Yo Ma, Pete Seeger, and U2 are some of the supporters. Other kids are doing fund-raisers too.

I think about the day when the statue of Mr. Smailovic will stand tall in Sarajevo. I thank Nanny for always believing in me and for understanding me, even when I was very young. It doesn't take an adult to make a difference, and it doesn't take a president to bring peace to the world. It all starts with us—kids—and it all starts right around us—in our homes, neighborhoods, schools, and communities. All we have to do is reach out to help somebody, and we become part of the solution instead of part of the problem.

Share Jason's dream for kids of the world to unite and work together for world peace. Contact: The Cello Cries On, Inc., 619 Rose Drive, Newburgh, Indiana 47630. Web site: **http://members.sigecom.net/jdc**.

CHAPTER 28

Q Studio Solo 1999

The Best of Both Worlds

MAIKO XIONG

IN MY CULTURE—THE HMONG CULTURE OF SOUTHEAST ASIA—boys are considered superior. When a boy marries, he and his wife must live with his mother and father and take care of them. Naturally, Hmong parents hope for sons.

I am one of eleven children. My brother is the oldest and the only boy. I know my parents were upset each time they had another girl. But I have never felt unloved.

When I was younger, I never understood my parents. They didn't "Americanize." I wondered why they wouldn't speak English, dress like Americans, or give up Asian customs.

Typical of our culture was my parents' strict nature. I was not allowed to go many places. I remember even having to ask to go to the park across the street.

I felt inferior to American kids. At times I wished I were one of them. Then I wouldn't be in a minority. I would look the same as them, and I could go and do what they got to do.

At school I was really shy, but I did feel comfortable with my Asian friends. We'd been together since elementary school. Some of them would go behind their parents' backs and go out. I wouldn't do that because I was too afraid my parents would find out. I just listened to stories about where my friends went and took in as much as I could.

About three months before I was going to graduate from junior high school, we moved. I had to go to a new high school—in Merced, California—and I didn't know one person. For me, a shy person anyway, this move about destroyed me.

Everyone was in cliques, and I just didn't fit in. I went to school early every day because my dad had to take me on his way to work. I would get out of the car and have nowhere to go. I would go into the school and sit in a corner. I'd get out a notebook and start writing just to look busy. This was the saddest time of my life. I lived alone in a world that frightened me.

One of my sisters was a junior in high school. She was a member of the Valley 4-H chapter in Merced County and invited me to a meeting. I always thought of 4-H as a club for white kids who liked cows and pigs. I wasn't really interested in going, but I went with her anyway because I didn't have anything else to do.

At the meeting I discovered all the kids in the chapter were Asians, and they weren't doing any projects with animals. They were working on community service projects and leadership programs. I signed up for every project there, just to keep busy. It was a new starting point in my life.

I became a part of the Read More Program. The former president of Valley 4-H had received a grant for the program, whose goal was to help underprivileged kids read better. We went to the Boys and Girls Club and to different underprivileged communities helping kids learn to read and having them read out loud to us.

Now, after school I had something to do, and it was so great, having those kids to work with. To help a child read and see his big smile after he read a story to me felt so good.

I suddenly had new friends. Not only the kids I was tutoring, but also other 4-H members I met through project meetings and leadership conferences. We worked together and enjoyed each other's company because we had the same interests and goals.

My friends were not just Asian. I had a group of friends from many different backgrounds—friends I met through 4-H.

I went to a 4-H conference in Washington, DC, with about 450 kids. The conference focused on good citizenship. I got to meet great people, see monuments, and go to museums. I can't imagine how my life may have turned out if I had not joined 4-H. I'm helping others, making lasting friendships, and feeling great about myself.

This past year—my senior year—I led the Read More Program. It's amazing to me how far I have come since my freshman year when I felt so isolated and inferior.

Recently my parents told me their immigration story. It wasn't the first time I heard it. But this time I heard it with different ears.

My parents fled to America in 1980 to get away from the Communist government of Laos. They left Laos with the clothes on their back, a fifty-pound bag of rice, and my brother and sister—their only children at the time. They walked for thirteen days. My mom didn't even own shoes. They reached Thailand and quietly crossed the Mekong River at night with my brother and sister on their backs. They didn't know if they would get caught. All they cared about was giving their children a better way of life.

When they got to America they had nothing. They were on welfare for a long time while they adjusted to a new life. My dad now works at the Lao Family Community Center helping people who don't understand English.

I felt a new sense of admiration for my parents as they spoke. They loved their homeland and sacrificed for us. Yet they wanted us to experience the beauty of Southeast Asian culture, so they never gave up their customs.

Having matured and come to a place of peace within myself, I am able to enjoy both Hmong culture and the American way. I have the best of both worlds!

We had a big feast for my high school graduation. I spent the night at my cousin's house, and we woke up around 3 A.M. to make rice like my mom made in Laos. We rinsed vegetables and waited for all the meat to arrive. We had the best time getting together, laughing, and talking about what's going on in everybody's life.

My parents have come a long way, too. They listen now when my sisters and I tell them we can help take care of them—it's not just my brother's responsibility. They're slowly understanding that it's OK for girls to go get an education, make a living, and maybe get married later in life.

My parents are proud I am entering Davis University. We all have learned so much about life during my high school years. We all know we're not giving anything up by accepting both Hmong and American culture into our lives—we're becoming better human beings.

If you're looking for a vehicle to help build skills for the meaningful development of youth and adults and communities, as well as a means of solidifying the mutual relationship and commitment of young people with community, contact: National 4-H Council, 7100 Connecticut Avenue, Chevy Chase, Maryland 20815. Tel: 301-961-2800. Fax: 301-961-2894. Web site: **www.fourhcouncil.edu**.

CHAPTER 29

More Than Meets the Eye

JORGE CEDILLO

THROUGHOUT ELEMENTARY, MIDDLE, AND HIGH SCHOOL, kids said I was fat and ugly. Whenever I changed clothes during P.E., kids looked at me and laughed. They talked about my hair, too, because I had a ponytail. A couple of times I got into fights, but most times I just walked away. It was senseless to fight.

My parents had their own problems. They were on welfare. We never stayed in one house very long—if the rent went up, we couldn't pay the bills. Sometimes we moved in with relatives until we could rent another house. I would start to make a friend around the neighborhood, then all of a sudden, we would move. It was hard on me. But my parents told me to always look at the positive side of a move. I may be losing a friend, but I was getting ready to meet a new one.

They never complained about not having money. More important to them were my sister's and my happiness. No matter how bad a day my mom was having, she always wanted to know how my day and my sister's day went. My mom always said, "You children come first. Your dad and I come second."

Sometimes I wished I had more stuff. But my parents told me to appreciate what I had—not to expect to get everything I want.

Many days I came home from school and my mom would look at me and ask me what was wrong. I didn't want to say anything to her. I just went to my room and lay down. I was depressed—I wished I didn't have to go to school because of all of the teasing.

I did have one good friend in middle school. Michael didn't care what I looked like. But then he went to a different high school than me, and I was on my own again. The teasing continued. Finally I got mad enough to want to prove to everyone that I was somebody—that I could lose weight. I showed up at the first football practice. The coach put me on the last string, since it was my first time to play football and I was so out of shape.

The first time I ran, I felt like dying. It was really hard, with all of the pads I had to wear and with me being overweight. Sweat poured out of me. But I kept going.

The more I practiced, the easier it became. And I started to lose weight. I liked the structured schedule and the discipline required, so I decided to join ROTC. I learned first aid, map reading, and marksmanship.

We sent mail to military personnel and gave Christmas presents to the homeless. I never thought doing a simple community service project could make me feel so good. Because my mom and my dad had so many money problems, I knew what receiving a present would mean to these children. But when we actually gave them the gifts and I saw the children's smiles, I never felt better. I knew I was somebody—somebody who could help others.

I lost thirty pounds. I got a job at Winn Dixie, and with my work money bought myself a weight bench. I put it in my backyard and lifted weights regularly. For the first time in my life, I felt powerful. My depression lifted, and my attitude about everything improved. Kids stopped teasing me and started hanging around me.

I stopped playing football last season so I could spend more time with ROTC. I participated in the Community Youth Development Project to improve my leadership skills in ROTC.

When it came time to choose a project, I immediately suggested we help the homeless. Our group decided to print a flyer that said,

> Did you know that the average age of the homeless in America is nine?
> There are over 18,000 people living in poverty in Sarasota County, Florida.

Fourteen percent of households earn the equivalent of $15,000 or less. Wage rates are 5 percent to 20 percent less than in most other southern metropolitan areas for the same jobs. Over 45 percent of the very low-income families who do rent have problems with defective housing or cost. On any given day in Sarasota County, approximately 1,300 people are homeless. In families with low incomes, abuse is 4.5 times more frequent, and neglect is nine times more frequent than in families with higher incomes. Most legal immigrants were ineligible for food stamps and SSI after August 1997.

On the bottom of the flyer it said, "Please help us help them by filling the bag with your contribution. Our group will return on Saturday, March 13, to collect your contributions. Please leave the bag outside. Any of the following items would help us in our attempt to help the homeless: toiletries, blankets, shoes, and socks." We put bags at the YMCA, grocery stores, schools, and at homes in our neighborhoods.

We got a great response. We took over $3,000 worth of items—five carloads full—to the Salvation Army and the Resurrection House, a shelter in Sarasota County.

My mom and dad are now off welfare. My dad is a cook, and my mom is a Health Unit coordinator. They feel more secure and are very thankful they have jobs. They tell me all of the time how proud they are of me—for losing weight and changing my attitude.

I tell them my attitude changed because she and my dad were there to help me, along with my friend, Michael. Another overweight teen getting teased—without any close relationships—might stay depressed and heartbroken. The situation could end like that incident in Colorado.

I really don't care about the past—just the future. There's a kid named Andreo who went to elementary school and middle school with me. He always teased me.

When we both played football our freshman year, he saw me losing weight. Just a few weeks ago another kid was talking about me. Andreo said, "Leave him alone. He has lost a lot of weight since he was in elementary school."

Andreo had apologized to me in his own way. For a moment it was hard to accept—he had really hurt me. But I'm not the kind of person who's going to hold grudges against people. I say, forgive and forget.

Need help deciding how you can best serve in your community? Contact: Community Youth Development Project, 4409 Sawyer Road, Sarasota, Florida 34233. Tel: 941-922-5126. Fax: 941-922-8099. Web site: **www.sarasota-YMCA.org**.

CHAPTER 30

Do Unto Others

LIZ GARSON

ABOUT SIX YEARS AGO WE WENT TO DINNER at our neighbor's home. Our host, Don, invited other neighbors too. My dad worked at night so he wasn't with us. When he got home and we weren't there, he got angry. He came down the street and banged on the door. It was locked, but he pushed the door open anyway. One of the women at the party happened to be leaving at that moment. The door swung open and hit her. My dad started hollering at everyone—it was some scene.

My mom called the police to settle him down. That was the night my dad got kicked out of the house. I wasn't really surprised. My parents fought all the time. But it still hurt knowing I wouldn't be living with both of them anymore.

We lived in Kensington, one of the worst neighborhoods in Philadelphia. If you walked outside my house, you might see someone selling drugs to people in cars as they drove past. From inside my house, my brother saw a guy he knew get shot. Guns, drugs, prostitution—you name it, it's there.

My mom wanted to leave the area, but she was on welfare and couldn't afford to. She started going out with Don, the neighbor who had us over for dinner. After a while, he asked my mom to move in with him.

Mom asked me and my older brother and sister if we had a problem moving in with him. They told her they liked him. I hated him with a passion, and I told her so.

I didn't like him, I didn't like the house—I didn't like anything having to do with the situation. You just get intuition about certain people. I felt uncomfortable around him.

We moved in with him anyway. There was nothing I could do.

My mom had my two little sisters with Don. He and I didn't really speak to each other unless he needed me to do something, like change my sisters' diapers.

My mother and Don never got married. Even though we lived together, he never paid any of the bills. He could have helped us; he was an auto mechanic. We had welfare coming in, but we were strapped for money.

We lived with him for two years. Last year Mom finally realized what he was really about and we moved out. We went to stay at my grandmother's in Bridesberg, a nicer neighborhood in Philly.

Meeting new friends at my age—fourteen—was a challenge. I stayed at my school in Kensington, but there were a whole new group of neighborhood kids to hang with. It's funny—we moved out of the most dangerous neighborhood into a much nicer area, and that's when I first tried drugs. It was a peer pressure thing. Everyone else was doing it, so I thought I'd fit into the new group if I joined in.

We got caught by one of the girl's parents. They blamed me because I was the "new girl." From then on I wasn't able to be with my new friend without her parents' supervision.

Kensington was supposed to be the worst neighborhood, but the neighbors were actually neighborly. They were hospitable and didn't go around acting like they were better off than I was. That was the feeling I got in Bridesberg.

I started cutting class and failed a few subjects. I finished out the school year where I was and then started at Frankford High School in September 1998.

In some ways things got a little better. I didn't do any more drugs and didn't cut class. My mom got a job and got off welfare. We were living with my grandmother, and I didn't have to worry about being around Don. But my older sister moved out to live with my father, and my older brother joined the Army. So it was up to me to help my grandmother with my younger sisters and brothers while my mom was at work. My younger brothers and sisters were now eleven, eight, five, and three years old.

I love them all, but baby-sitting and cleaning the house was not the greatest life for me. I didn't have anything in my life to look forward to, to enjoy, or to make me feel good about myself.

A teacher at Frankford changed all of that. He came up to me at school and told me it was mandatory that I get community service hours in order to graduate. He thought I would like a new project at our school called Fashionably Frankford. He told me I needed to go check it out.

What started out as a way to earn service hours became a way for me to begin to live and not just exist. A group of us met, and Rachel, the twenty-five-year-old adviser, explained the project to a group of us.

She told us, "You are starting a unique project from the ground up. Fashionably Frankford is a store you're going to open offering men and women free clothing for their jobs as they move from welfare to work. The clothes come from private donations. A client can come in when they're in a job-training program to get interview-appropriate clothes. They can come back one more time after they get a job to get the attire they need for work. You need to come up with a logo, paint this room, learn how to sort inventory, learn how to do spreadsheets, and track the client from when he or she comes in for the first time to when they come back for follow-up."

We looked around at the horrendous room we were meeting in and knew what we needed to do first. We painted the room blue because our school colors are blue, red, and yellow. One of the students made a banner with the logo we decided on: Fashionably Frankford—Dress to Impress for Success.

We received display racks to hang the clothes from Frankford Group Ministry.

Teachers donated clothes and corporations sent clothes. Our principal even contacted his tailor, and he donated clothing. We never held any clothing drives— we had plenty of clothes to open the store. We sized the clothes, put them on hangers, and arranged them on racks just like a real store. We even got shopping bags donated from Acme.

In one month we learned how to start a business and how to make it look awesome. Our adviser, Rachel, couldn't believe what we had accomplished. We decided our store hours would be three days a week for three hours each day. Rachel trained us on the procedures we needed to follow with each client.

Then we were ready to open the store. Different welfare-to-work programs— Frankford Group Ministry, Frankford Job Bank, Jewish Employment Ventures, to name a few—referred clients to us.

I'll never forget the first client I helped. I walked outside to meet her and to get her paperwork from her referral agency. I took her to the store and found her size. I told her to pick out one business suit and one dress or pants and a blouse. She went into a private area we used as the dressing room.

She came out looking beautiful. I told her how nice she looked. You should have seen her smile when she looked in the mirror and saw herself.

Since that day our store has served hundreds of men and women in our community. We've gotten press coverage—even the NBA honored us. We developed a free start-up kit for other students in the United States. Our hope is that other schools will have stores and will contribute to the success of their communities.

All of us working together in the store are the best of friends—including Rachel. She puts her heart and soul into this project and into us. I can tell her anything because she understands teenagers so well.

The good feeling I got from helping my first client probably changed me more than anything else ever has. Knowing I was making a difference in someone's life made my life worthwhile. I guess it's the old rule kicking in—do unto others as you would have done to you—with a new meaning for me. Do unto others as you would have done to you, and you really will have it done to you!

Provide clothing for welfare-to-work men and women in your community. Contact Fashionably Frankford for your free start-up kit for your school. Fashionably Frankford, P. O. Box 23046, Philadelphia, Pennsylvania 19124. Tel: 215-537-2519 Ext. 4000.

] WANT TO THANK ALL OF THE WONDERFUL PEOPLE WHO HELPED with the development of this book. First, and foremost, my heartfelt thanks to Steve, my husband of twenty-eight years, for the love we have known and for the love we have been enabled to give. My love and thanks to our children, Melissa, Todd, and Michael, whose humor and insight guide me daily. And I'm grateful to our parents for their love, support, and involvement in our lives.

A special thanks goes to Dallas Public Schools for their guidance with the Group Discussion Guide. Their recommendation of the curriculum, *Discover: Skills for Life,* American Guidance Service, Inc., aided me in my research. I am ever grateful to the Peel District School Board in Ontario for their contribution to the Canadian resources in the Resource Guide and for suggesting I profile Talli Osborne. I thank the National Association of Secondary School Principals (NASSP) for the resources they recommend on their web site, some of which I included in the book.

My thanks to Judy Williams for transcribing hours of conversation in record time. This project would not have been possible without the organizational skills of Larissa Khatain, my dynamic teen-assistant from Allen, Texas. Her Excel charts, files, and reminder notes kept me on track all summer. I'll never forget the day she handed me written pages of her story, letting me know what she had gone through and how she had heard the call to action. I've learned a lot from her.

I want to thank Cassie Carroll for sharing her story with me, and for showing me just how courageous we can be when we choose to be.

This book would not have been possible without the help of the dedicated individuals working at the nonprofits where these teens are helping others. Their enthusiasm, passion, and tireless efforts are making a difference—these teens are shining reflections of their hard work and caring attitudes. I thank them for giving me the help I asked for.

Thanks goes to Jim Levine, the agent who never sleeps, answers e-mails within minutes, and whose intelligence, integrity, and advice I greatly value. I appreciate all that Karen Frost, publicist extraordinaire, has done to get the word out.

Thanks to Will, Brenda, Heather, Sharon, Rosie, Jenny, Suzanne, Teresa, and the entire family at Conari; this book went way beyond my wildest hopes and dreams. I thank them for giving the teens' voices a magnificent platform.

Who gets to have their manuscript edited three times? Who is told, "You can do this, believe in yourself." Mary Jane Ryan, copublisher and executive editor of Conari Press, made this book possible. Without her brilliant editing, encouragement, and generosity of spirit, I could never have completed this book. I am grateful.

I thank each of the teens profiled in the book for sharing their story, so that we all may know how to have the courage to give.

Everybody can be great ... because anybody can serve.
You don't have to have a college degree to serve. You don't have
to make your subject and verb agree to serve. You only need
a heart full of grace. A soul generated by love.

—*Martin Luther King, Jr.*

1. Which personal story touched you the most? Why?

2. Which story could you best relate to? What part of the story helped you the most?

3. All these teens discovered that helping others helped them. What changed in their lives to make them feel this way?

4. Each of the stories concludes with the teen sharing what they have learned from their experience. Which story caused you to think of life in a different way?

5. The teens' stories emphasize the importance of communication—talking with someone, letting feelings out rather than holding emotions inside. If you have a problem and don't feel comfortable telling someone you know, what could you do?

6. If you decide to share your problem with a trusting adult or take steps to increase your safety, you are taking charge of your own welfare. What can this lead to?

7. If you feel comfortable talking about your problem with someone you feel close to, name two adults in your life, other than a parent, to whom you can go.

8. When should you seek help with problem situations?

9. What happens when your perspective is one of helplessness?

10. What happens when your perspective is one of hopefulness?

11. What does this statement mean to you: It's not what happens to you; it's what you do about it.

12. What are your needs, wants, and values? How do they affect your decision making?

13. How do outside influences—family, peers, media—influence your decision making?

14. What are your personal goals?

15. Do the decisions you make help you achieve your goals?

16. If someone is having a problem and comes to you for help, how can you help him or her?

17. When someone shares their problem with you and trusts you to keep secret what they tell you, when is it appropriate to tell a professional or other adult?

18. Share a time when you were in pain and chose to reach out and help someone, putting aside your own problem for the moment. Describe how you felt afterward.

19. Some of the teens in the book express gratitude toward a friend, teacher, or an adult for guiding them in a direction that gave their life meaning. In what ways were they guided?

20. These teens feel the root cause of teenage problems is the need for acceptance. Some suggestions for promoting acceptance in schools include initiation of the "I Will Pledge," a welcome committee or buddy system for new students, peer mediation, and an acceptance campaign for the school year. What is your school doing to promote acceptance? How can you help?

21. Develop a call to action plan for yourself, your class, or your school. Discover your individual and collective strengths by asking:

   • Do I (we) connect best with children, peers, or senior citizens?

   • Have I (we) had a life-changing experience that I (we) can use to help others?

   • Do I (we) have specific talents or interests I (we) can share with others?

   • What kind of issues and needs motivate me (us)?

HAVE THE COURAGE TO GIVE. Use the resource guide provided in this book or resources available at your school.

Conflict Resolution

Never give up on anybody.

—*Hubert H. Humphrey*

Bureau for At-Risk Youth
645 New York Avenue
Huntington, New York 11743
Tel: 800-99-YOUTH
Fax: 516-673-4544

**Children's Creative Response to
Conflict**
Box 271, 523 North Broadway
Nyack, New York 10960
Tel: 914-358-4601
Fax: 914-358-4924

Domestic Abuse Awareness Project
P. O. Box 1155
Madison Square Station
New York, New York 10159-1155
Tel: 212-529-5641

**Future Wave (Working for Alternatives
to Violence through Entertainment)**
2020 Productions, Inc.
105 Camino Teresa
Santa Fe, New Mexico 87505-4703
Tel: 505-982-8882
Fax: 505-982-6460

Juvenile Justice Clearinghouse
P. O. Box 6000
Rockville, Maryland 20849-6000
Tel: 800-638-8736
Fax: 301-519-5212
E-mail: askncjrs@ncjrs.org

National Association for Mediation in Education (NAME)
425 Amity Street
Amherst, Massachusetts 01002
Tel: 413-545-2462
Fax: 413-545-4802

National Coalition against Domestic Violence
P. O. Box 34103
Washington, DC 20043-4103
Tel: 202-638-6388

National Council on Child Abuse and Family Violence
1155 Connecticut Avenue NW, Suite 300
Washington, DC 20036
Tel: 800-222-2000

National Crime Prevention Council
Municipal and Youth Initiative Unit
1700 K Street, NW, 2d Floor
Washington, DC 20006
Tel: 202-466-6272

National Youth Network
OJJDP
810 7th Street, NW
Washington, DC 20531
Tel: 202-307-5911
Fax: 202-307-2093
E-mail: askjj@ojp.usdpj.gov

Peace Education Foundation
1900 Biscayne Boulevard
Miami, Florida 33132

Students Against Violence Everywhere (SAVE)
Executive Director: Gary Weart
Center for the Prevention of School Violence
20 Enterprise Street, Suite 2
Raleigh, North Carolina 27607
Tel: 800-299-6054
Fax: 919-515-9397
Web site: **www.ncsu.edu/cpsv/**

Prevention Programs

Be sure you put your feet in the right place, then stand firm.
—*Abraham Lincoln*

Canadian Centre on Drug Prevention
75 Albert Street, Suite 300
Ottawa, Ontario K1P 5E7 Canada
Tel: 613-235-4048
Fax: 613-235-8101

CAVEAT (Canadians Against Violence Everywhere Advocating Its Termination)
3350 Fairview Street, Suite 3-164
Burlington, Ontario L7N3L5 Canada
Tel: 800-622-8328
Fax: 905-632-3039
Web site: **www.caveat.org**

Center for Substance Abuse Prevention
Teen Drinking Prevention Program
820 1st Street NE, #510
Washington, DC 20002
Tel: 800-937-6727
Tel: 202-408-5556

The Center for Tobacco-Free Kids
1707 L Street NW, Suite 800
Washington, DC 20036
Tel: 800-284-KIDS
Tel: 202-296-5469
Fax: 202-296-5427
E-mail: info@tobaccofreekids.org

Free the Children
1750 Steeles Avenue West, Suite 218
Concord, Ontario L4K 2L7
Canada
Tel: 905-760-9382
Fax: 905-760-9157
E-mail: freechild@clo.com

"Just Say No" International
President: Ivy Cohen
2101 Webster Street, Suite 1300
Oakland, California 94612
Tel: 800-258-2766
Tel: 510-451-6666
Fax: 510-451-9360

Students To Stop Peer Pressure (STOPP)
Sponsor: STOPP Consulting Services
Executive Director: Peter Jean
P. O. Box 103
Hudson, New Hampshire 03051-0103
Tel: 603-889-8163

Hotlines

You yourself, as much as anybody in the entire universe,
deserve your love and affection.
—*Buddha*

Agoraphobic Foundation
Tel: 514-688-4726

Al-Anon/Alateen Family Group Headquarters
Tel: 800-344-2666 (United States), 800-443-4525 (Canada)

Alcohol Treatment Referral Hotline
Tel: 800-ALCOHOL

Anonymous Sexual Abuse Recovery
Tel: 905-765-5769

Bilingual AIDS Hotline
Tel. 800-400-7432

Bulimia-Anorexia Association
Tel: 519-253-7545

Canadian Society for the Investigation of Child Abuse
Tel: 403-289-8385

CDC AIDS Info
Tel: 800-342-2437

Center for Substance Abuse Treatment
Tel: 800-662-HELP

Cocaine Hotline
Tel: 800-COCAINE

Emergency Contraception Hotline
Tel: 888-NOT-2LATE

Institute of the Prevention of Child Abuse
Tel: 800-888-KIDZ

Kids Help Phone–Canada
Tel: 800-668-6868

Marijuana Anonymous World Services
Tel: 800-766-6779

Multilingual AIDS Information and Referral Line
Tel: 800-922-2438

NAPARE Alcohol, Drug, and Pregnancy Hotline
Tel: 800-638-BABY

Narcotics Anonymous
Tel: 818-773-9999

National AIDS Clearinghouse
Tel: 800-458-5231

National AIDS Hotline
Tel: 800-342-AIDS

National Child Abuse Hotline
Tel: 800-422-4453

National Council on Alcoholism and Drug Dependence
Tel: 800-622-2255

National Drug Abuse Hotline
Tel: 800-662-4357

National Runaway Hotline
Tel: 800-621-4000

National Hotline for Missing and Exploited Children
Tel: 800-843-5678

STD Info Line
Tel: 800-227-8922

Teen Help
Tel: 800-840-5704

Youth Crisis Hotline
Tel: 800-448-4663

Online Resources

> Some people see things as they are and ask why.
> I dream things that never were and ask why not.
> —*Robert F. Kennedy*

City Kids
Web site: www.citykids.com

E-Teen
Web site: www.e-teen.org

Idealist
Web site: www.idealist.org

Impact Online
Web site: www.volunteermatch.org

Kids Health
Web site: www.kidshealth.org

Not Me, Not Now
Web site: www.notmenotnow.org

Youth Service America
Web site: www.servenet.org

SHINE (Seeking Harmony in Neighborhoods)
Web site: www.shinesite.org

Teenwire
Web site: www.teenwire.com

Safe Place Agencies

> History, although sometimes made up of the few acts of the great,
> is more often shaped by the many acts of the small.
>
> —*Mark Twain*

Big Brothers and Big Sisters of America
Tel: 215-567-7000

Big Brothers and Big Sisters of Canada
3228 South Service Road, Suite 113E
Burlington, Ontario L7N 3H8
Canada
Tel: 800-263-9133

Boys and Girls Clubs of America
Tel: 404-815-5700

Boys and Girls Clubs of Canada
National Office/Bureau national:
7100 Woodbine Avenue, Suite 405
Markham, Ontario L3R 5G2
Canada
Tel: 905-477-7272

Camp Fire Boys and Girls
Executive Director: K. Russell
   Weathers
4601 Madison Avenue
Kansas City, Missouri 64112-1278

Tel: 816-756-1950
Fax: 816-756-0258
E-mail: hn4395@handsnet.org

Girl Guides of Canada
50 Merton Street
Toronto, Ontario, M4S 1A3
Canada
E-mail: ggc@girlguide.ca
Web site: **www.girlguides.ca**

Scouts Canada
Tel: 1-888-ScoutsNow!
   (888-726-8876)
Web site: **www.scouts.ca**

YMCA of the USA
101 North Wacker Drive
Chicago, Illinois 60606
Tel: 312-977-0031
Fax: 312-977-9063
Web site: **www.ymca.net**

YWCA of the USA
Empire State Building
350 Fifth Avenue, Suite 301
New York, New York 10118
Tel: 212-273-7800
Fax: 212-465-2281
Web site: **www.ywca.org**

Community Service Organizations

Ask not what your country can do for you, ask what you
can do for your country.
—*John F. Kennedy*

The Giraffe Project
P .O. Box 759
197 Second Street
Langley, Washington 98260
Tel: 360-221-7989
Web site: **www.giraffe.org/giraffe/**

National Council of Volunteer Centers
Tel: 800-VOLUNTEER

The Salvation Army United States
Tel: 800-Sal-ARMY
Web site: **www.savationarmyusa.org**

The Salvation Army Canada
Tel: 888-321-3433

Save the Children
54 Wilton Road
Westport, Connecticut 06880
Tel: 800-243-5075
Web site: **www.savethechildren.org**

Volunteers of America
Tel: 703-548-2288

Volunteer Canada
Tel: 800-670-0401

Youth Service America
1101 15th Street, NW, Suite 200
Washington, DC 20005
Tel: 202-296-2992
Web site: **www.ysa.org**

I keep my ideals, because in spite of everything, I still believe
that people are really good at heart.
—*Anne Frank*

Barrymore, Drew. *Little Girl Lost*. New York: Pocket Books, 1991.

Canfield, Jack, et al. *Chicken Soup for the Teenage Soul*. Deerfield Beach: Health Communications, Inc., 1997.

_____. *Chicken Soup for the Teenage Soul II: 101 More Stories of Life, Love and Learning*. Deerfield Beach: Health Communications, Inc., 1998.

Carlip, Hillary. *Girl Power: Young Women Speak Out*. New York: Warner, 1995.

Covey, Sean. *The 7 Habits of Highly Effective Teens: The Ultimate Teenage Success Guide*. New York: Simon and Shuster, 1998.

Frank, Anne. *Anne Frank: The Diary of a Young Girl*. New York: Bantam Books, 1993.

Gootman, Marilyn E. *When a Friend Dies: A Book for Teens about Grieving and Healing*. Minneapolis: Free Spirit Publishing, Inc., 1994.

Gravelle, Karen and Haskins, Charles. *Teenagers Face to Face with Bereavement*. Messner, 1989.

Kirberger, Kimberly. *Teen Love: On Relationships*. Deerfield Beach: Health Communications, Inc., 1999.

Levy, Barrie. *In Love and In Danger: A Teen's Guide to Breaking Free of Abusive Relationships*. Seattle: Seal Press, 1998.

Lowry, Lois. *The Giver.* New York: Bantam Doubleday Dell Publishing Group, Inc., 1993.

Magorian, Michelle. *Goodnight, Mr. Tom.* New York: HarperCollins, 1981.

Peck, M. Scott, M.D. *The Road Less Traveled.* New York: Simon and Schuster, 1985.

Pipher, Mary, M.D. *Reviving Ophelia.* New York: Ballantine Books, 1994.

Random Acts of Kindness.™ Berkeley: Conari Press, 1993.

Rawls, Wilson. *Summer of the Monkeys.* New York: Bantam Books, 1976.

Shandler, Sara. *Ophelia Speaks: Adolescent Girls Write about Their Search for Self.* New York: HarperPerennial, 1999.

Silverstein, Shel. *Falling Up.* New York: HarperCollins Publishers, 1996.

Soto, Gary. *Buried Onions.* New York: HarperCollins Juvenile Books, 1997.

Traisman, Enid. *Fire in My Heart, Ice in My Veins.* Centering Corporation, 1992.

Vanzant, Iyanla. *Don't Give It Away.* New York: Fireside, 1999.

Wilmer, Bruce. *Believe in Yourself: Poems of Purpose.* Huntington: Wilmer Graphics, Inc. 1998.

Youngs, Bettie, et al. *Taste Berries for Teens: Inspirational Short Stories and Encouragement on Life, Love, Friendship and Tough Issues.* Deerfield Beach: Health Communications, Inc., 1999.

Youngholm, Thomas. *The Celestial Bar.* Creative Information Concepts, 1995.

THE AUTHOR OF *COURAGE TO GIVE*, JACKIE WALDMAN is the co-founder of Dallas' Random Acts of Kindness Week™ and has volunteered for the Multiple Sclerosis Society, the March of Dimes, the National Council of Jewish Women, and the Dallas Memorial Center for Holocaust Studies. A recipient of Girl's Inc.'s 1999 "She Knows Where She's Going" Award, Jackie is also a member of the advisory board for Our Friend's Place, a safe haven for abused girls. She lives in Dallas, Texas, with her husband, three children, and two dogs.

If you have ever faced a physical or emotional obstacle in your life, reached out to help others and learned that by helping others, you ultimately helped yourself, I want to hear from you. Contact me at my website at: www.couragetogive.com

To Our Readers

Conari Press publishes books on topics ranging from spirituality, personal growth, and relationships to women's issues, parenting, and social issues. Our mission is to publish quality books that will make a difference in people's lives—how we feel about ourselves and how we relate to one another. We value integrity, compassion, and receptivity, both in the books we publish and in the way we do business.

As a member of the community, we sponsor the Random Acts of Kindness™ Foundation, the guiding force behind Random Acts of Kindness™ Week. We donate our damaged books to nonprofit organizations, dedicate a portion of our proceeds from certain books to charitable causes, and continually look for new ways to use natural resources as wisely as possible.

Our readers are our most important resource, and we value your input, suggestions, and ideas about what you would like to see published. Please feel free to contact us, to request our latest book catalog, or to be added to our mailing list.

CONARI PRESS
2550 Ninth Street, Suite 101
Berkeley, California 94710-2551
800-685-9595   510-649-7175
fax: 510-649-7190   e-mail: conari@conari.com
www.conari.com